Principles of Accounting

D1412283

Online Diagnostic Test

Go to **Schaums.com** to launch the Schaum's Diagnostic Test.

This convenient application provides a 30-question multiple-choice test that will pinpoint areas of strength and weakness to help you focus your study. Questions cover all aspects of beginning chemistry, and the correct answers are explained in full. With a question-bank that rotates daily, the Schaum's Online Test also allows you to check your progress and readiness for final exams.

Other titles featured in Schaum's Online Diagnostic Test:

Principles of Accounting

Joel J. Lerner, Ph.D.
James A. Cashin, CPA

Abridgement Editor:
Daniel L. Fulks, Ph.D.

New York Chicago San Francisco Lisbon London Madrid Mexico City
Milan New Delhi San Juan Seoul Singapore Sydney Toronto

The McGraw·Hill Companies

JOEL J. LERNER is retired professor and former chairman of the business division at Sullivan County Community College in New York. He received his B.S. from New York University and his M.S. and Ph.D. from Columbia University. He has written several *Schaum's Outlines* and lectures widely on finance.

JAMES A. CASHIN was emeritus professor of Accounting at Hofstra University. He held a B.S. in Accounting from the University of Georgia and M.B.A. from New York University. He was also a Certified Public Accountant and a Certified Internal Auditor.

DANIEL L. FULKS is associate professor and director of the Accounting Program at Transylvania University in Lexington, Kentucky. He received his B.S. degree from the University of Tennessee, an M.B.A. from the University of Maryland, and a Ph.D. from Georgia State University. He is also a Certified Public Accountant. He previously taught at the University of Kentucky and worked in private business for several years. He is the abridgement editor for *Schaum's Easy Outlines: Principles of Accounting* and co-editor for *Schaum's Easy Outlines: Business Statistics*.

1 2 3 4 5 6 7 8 9 10 11 12 13 14 15   DOC/DOC   1 9 8 7 6 5 4 3 2 1

ISBN   978-0-07177752-0
MHID   0-07-177752-0

McGraw-Hill books are available at special quantity discounts to use as premiums and sales promotions or for use in corporate training programs. To contact a representative, please e-mail us at bulksales@mcgraw-hill.com.

This book is printed on acid-free paper.

Contents

Chapter 1
ACCOUNTING CONCEPTS:
THE ACCOUNTING EQUATION
AND FINANCIAL STATEMENTS

IN THIS CHAPTER:

✔ *Nature of Accounting*
✔ *Basic Elements of Financial Position and the Accounting Equation*
✔ *Financial Statements*
✔ *The Income Statement*
✔ *The Balance Sheet*
✔ *The Statement of Owner's Equity*
✔ *Classified Financial Statements*
✔ *Rules Governing Financial Statements*
✔ *Summary*
✔ *Solved Problems*

1

Nature of Accounting

Every element of society—from the individual to an entire industry or government branch—has to make decisions on how to allocate its resources. Accounting is the process that aids these decisions by recording, classifying, summarizing, and reporting business transactions and interpreting their effects on the affairs of the business entity.

Basic Elements of Financial Position: The Accounting Equation

The financial condition or position of a business enterprise is represented by the relationship of assets to liabilities and capital:

Assets. Properties used in business that are owned and have monetary value, for instance, cash, inventory, buildings, and equipment.

Liabilities. Amounts owed to creditors, including all payable accounts. Liabilities may also include certain deferred items.

Owner's Equity. The interest of the owners in an enterprise.

These three basic elements are connected by a fundamental relationship called the accounting equation. This equation expresses the equality of the assets on one side with the claims of the creditors and owners on the other side:

$$\textbf{Assets} = \textbf{Liabilities} + \textbf{Owner's Equity}$$

Remember

The accounting equation of Assets = Liabilities + Owner's Equity should balance after every transaction.

Example 1.1

During the month of January, Mr. Brent Gilfedder, lawyer,

1. Invested $5,000 to open his law practice
2. Bought office supplies on account, $500
3. Received $2,000 in fees earned during the month
4. Paid $100 on the account for the office supplies
5. Withdrew $500 for personal use

These transactions could be analyzed and recorded as follows:

Assets	=	Liabilities	+	Owner's Equity
Cash				Gilfedder, Capital
(1) + $5,000	=			+ $5,000
Supplies		Accounts Payable		
(2) + $500	=	+ $500		
Cash				Fees Income
(3) + $2,000				+ $2,000
Cash		Accounts Payable		
(4) − $100	=	− $100		
Cash				Gilfedder, Capital
(5) − $500	=			− $500

Notice that for every transaction, two entries are made. After every transaction, the accounting equation remains balanced.

Financial Statements

The simple balance of assets against liabilities and owner's equity is insufficient to give complete answers. Investors and creditors alike are interested in viewing the amount and type of both income items and expense items. They are also interested in viewing the amount and type of assets, liabilities, and owner's equity at the end of the period. In order to fulfill these desires, financial statements are provided. These financial statements include (1) the income statement, (2) the balance sheet, and (3) the statement of owner's equity.

The Income Statement

The income statement may be defined as a *summary of the revenue, expenses, and net income or net loss of a business entity for a specific period of time.* This may also be called a profit and loss statement, operating statement, or statement of operations. Let us review the meanings of the elements entering into the income statement:

Revenue. The increase in capital resulting from the sale of goods or rendering of services by the business. In amount, the revenue is equal to the cash, accounts receivable, or other assets gained in compensation for the goods sold or services rendered.

Expenses. The decrease in capital caused by the business's revenue-producing operations. In amount, the expense is equal to the value of goods and services used up or consumed in obtaining revenue.

Net Income. The increase in capital resulting from profitable operation of a business. It is the excess of revenues over expenses for the accounting period.

Net Loss. The decrease in capital resulting from the operations of a business. It is the excess of expenses over revenue for the accounting period.

It is important to note that a cash receipt qualifies as revenue only if it serves to increase capital. Thus, for instance, borrowing cash from a bank does not contribute to revenue. Similarly, a cash payment is an expense only if it decreases capital.

In many companies there are hundreds and perhaps thousands of income and expense transactions in one month. To lump all these transactions under one account would be very cumbersome and would, in addition, make it impossible to show relationships among the various items. For example, we might wish to know the relationship of selling expenses to sales and whether the ratio is higher or lower than in previous periods. To solve this problem, we leave the investment or permanent entries in the capital account and then set up a *temporary* set of income and expense accounts. The net difference of these accounts, the net profit or net loss, is then transferred as one figure to the capital account.

Because an income statement pertains to a definite period of time, it becomes necessary to determine just *when* an item of revenue or expense is to be accounted for. Under the *accrual basis of accounting,* revenue is recognized only when actually earned (as opposed to when received) and expense is recognized only when incurred (as opposed to paid.) This differs significantly from the *cash basis of accounting*, which recognizes revenue and expense generally with the receipt and payment of cash. Essential to the accrual basis is the *matching* of expenses with the revenue that they help produce. Under the accrual system, the accounts are adjusted at the end of the accounting period to properly reflect the revenue earned and the costs and expenses applicable to the period.

Most business firms use the accrual basis, while individuals and professional people generally use the cash basis. Ordinarily the cash basis is not suitable when there are significant amounts of inventories, receivables, and payables.

The Balance Sheet

The information needed for the balance sheet items consists of the net balances at the end of the period, rather than the total for the period, as in the income statement. Thus, management wants to know the balance of cash in the bank and the balance of inventory, equipment, etc., on hand at the end of the period.

The balance sheet may then be defined as a *statement showing the assets, liabilities, and owner's equity of a business entity at a specific date.* This statement is also called a statement of financial position or statement of financial condition.

Note!

In preparing the balance sheet, it is not necessary to make any further analysis of the data. The needed data, that is, the balance of the asset, liability, and owner's equity accounts, are already available.

The close relationship of the income statement and the balance sheet is apparent. The income statement is the connecting link between two balance sheets, the previous year and the current year. As discussed earlier, the income and expense items are actually a further analysis of the capital account.

The Statement of Owner's Equity

Instead of showing the details of the owner's equity account in the balance sheet, we may show the changes in a separate form called the statement of owner's equity. This is the more common treatment. The statement of owner's equity begins with the balance of the capital account on the first day of the period, adds increases in owner's equity (example: net income), and subtracts decreases in owner's equity (example: withdrawals) to reach the balance of the owner's equity account at the end of the period.

The Statement of Cash Flows

The statement of cash flows shows the sources (inflows) of cash and the uses (outflows) of cash for the entity for a given period. The net increase or decrease in the entity's cash balance during the period is summarized in three categories: operating activities, investing activities, and financing activities. The operating activities include the income generated and the expenses incurred in the normal business activities of the entity. Investing activities include cash used in acquiring the entity's assets and cash received from selling such assets. Financing activities include cash generated by debt, such as bank loans, and from selling shares of ownership. The statement of cash flows must reconcile the cash balances reflected on the balance sheets at the beginning and end of the entity's reporting period.

Financial Statement Summary

Income Statement
Month of January 20X1

Fees Income		$2,000
Expenses		
Rent Expense	$500	
Salaries Expense	200	
Supplies Expense	200	
Total Expenses		900
Net Income		$1,100

Statement of Owner's Equity
Month of January 20X1

Capital, January 1, 20X1		$5,000
Add: Net Income	$1,100	
Less: Drawing	(300)	
Increase in Capital		800
Capital, January 31, 20X1		$5,800

Balance Sheet
January 31, 20X1

Assets	
Cash	$4,700
Supplies	100
Equipment	2,500
Total Assets	$7,300

Liabilities and Owner's Equity

Accounts Payable	$1,500
Capital, January 31, 20X1	5,800
Total Liabilities and Owner's Equity	$7,300

Statement of Cash Flows
Month of January 20X1

Cash Flows from Operating Activities:

Receipts:			
Collections from Customers		$2,000	
Interest Received on Notes Receivable		200	$2,200
Payments:			
To Suppliers	1,000		
To Employees	500	1,500	
Net Cash Inflow from Operating Activities			700

Cash Flows from Investing Activities:

Acquisition of Plant Assets	(500)	
Proceeds from Sale of Investments	100	
Net Cash Outflow from Investing Activities		(400)

Cash Flows from Financing Activities:

Proceeds from Sale of Common Stock	2,000	
Payment of Notes Payable	(1,500)	
Net Cash Inflow from Financing Activities		500

Net Increase in Cash During Period

Cash Balance, January 1, 20X1	4,200	
Cash Balance, January 31, 20X1		$4,700

Remember

The four primary financial statements are:
- Balance Sheet
- Income Statement
- Statement of Owner's Equity
- Statement of Cash Flows

Classified Financial Statements: Balance Sheet

Financial statements become more useful when the individual items are classified into significant groups for comparison and financial analysis. The classifications relating to the balance sheet will be discussed in this section, while the classification of the income statement will be shown in a later chapter.

The balance sheet becomes a more useful statement for comparison and financial analysis if the asset and liability groups are classified. For example, an important index of the financial state of a business, derivable from the classified balance sheet, is the ratio of current assets to current liabilities. This *current ratio* should generally be at least 2:1; that is, current assets should be twice current liabilities. For our purpose, we will designate the following classifications:

Assets	Liabilities
Current	Current
Fixed	Long-Term
Other	Contingent

Assets include the following:

Current Assets. Assets reasonably expected to be converted into cash or used in the current operation of the business (generally taken as one year). Examples are cash, notes receivable, accounts receivable, inventory, and prepaid expenses.

Fixed Assets or Plant Assets. Long-lived assets used in the production of goods or services. These assets are used in the operation of the business rather than being held for sale, as are inventory items.

Other Assets. Various assets other than current assets, fixed assets, or assets to which specific captions are given. For instance, the caption Investments would be used if significant sums were invested. Often companies show a caption for intangible assets such as patents or goodwill. In other cases, there may be a separate caption for deferred charges. If, however, the amounts are not large in relation to total assets, the various items may be grouped under one caption, Other Assets.

Liabilities may be current, long-term, or contingent.

Current Liabilities. These are liabilities that are due for payment within the operating cycle or one year, whichever is longer. The settlement of a current liability usually requires the use of current assets. The ration of current assets to current liabilities, or current ratio, is a useful index of a company's debt-paying capacity.

Following are the seven principal types of current liabilities:

1. *Notes payable.* Liabilities evidenced by a written promise to pay at a later date.
2. *Accounts payable.* Liabilities for goods or services purchased on account, trade payables, and also nontrade obligations.
3. *Accrued liabilities.* Liabilities that have accumulated but are not yet due, as payment does not coincide with the end of the period. These are *expenses* and are shown on the income statement under

Salaries and Wages	Payroll Taxes
Commissions	Sales Taxes
Insurance	Income Taxes
Interest	Pensions
Property Taxes	Royalties

4. *Withholdings.* Amounts that have been withheld from employees' pay and are to be turned over to government agencies, insurance companies, etc. These are *not* expenses of the company but must be properly safeguarded until they are transmitted to the specified agency. These include income taxes, social security taxes, unemployment taxes, hospitalization, group insurance, and pensions.

5. *Dividends payable.* Dividends become payable only as declared by the board of the company. They do not accrue, or accumulate, as does interest on bonds.

6. *Unearned revenues.* Sometimes revenue is received in advance, such as magazine subscriptions or rent. These are liabilities, as they represent claims against the enterprise. Generally they are settled by delivery of goods or services in the next accounting period. Where these are long-term advances extending well beyond the next period, they should be classed on the balance sheet as noncurrent.

7. *Portion of long-term debt.* The portion of long-term debt payable in the next 12 months should be included in the current liabilities category. This includes amounts due on bonds, mortgages, or long-term notes.

Long-Term Liabilities. Where funds are needed for a long-term purpose such as construction of a building, a long-term liability account would be used. Presumably, increased earnings would be used to retire the debt. Almost always, long-term liabilities are interest-bearing and have a fixed due date.

Following are the principal types of long-term liabilities:

1. *Long-term notes payable.* The company may be able to obtain the needed amount from one lender rather than by issuing bonds for sale to the public. Sometimes notes may be issued to await better terms for issuing bonds.

2. *Mortgages payable.* The terms of a mortgage generally pledge the property of a company as security. The mortgage involves a lien on the property, but not a transfer of title.

3. *Bonds payable.* If the amount of funds needed is larger than a single lender can supply, bonds may be sold to the investing public, splitting the loan into thousands of units. A bond is a written promise to pay the face amount, generally $1,000, at a future date and to make interest payments semiannually at a stipulated rate of interest. Interest payments on bonds are deductible as expense for income tax purposes, but dividends paid on

preferred or common stock are not. This is an important consideration in deciding whether to use stocks or bonds for long-term financing.

Contingent Liabilities. These are potential liabilities arising from past events. For example, when a note receivable is endorsed and transferred to another person, no liability is created. However, there is a possibility that a liability could exist in the future, because the maker of the note may not honor it. If that were to happen, the business that endorsed the note would be required to make payment. Some other examples of contingent liabilities are additional tax assessments, product guarantees, pending lawsuits, and litigation.

You Need to Know

It is not necessary to prepare an entry until the potential liability becomes an actuality. However, it cannot be ignored. Therefore, a contingent liability should be reflected in the financial statements in a footnote describing the possibility of the loss. This will give the reader a more accurate picture of the financial position of the firm.

Rules Governing Financial Statements

Clearly, consistent rules must exist, for otherwise it would be necessary to state for each financial statement the specific assumptions used in preparing it. Over the years, certain principles have been developed on the basis of experience, reason, custom, and practical necessity. We call these *generally accepted accounting principles*, better known as GAAP.

> *Business entity.* Accounts are kept for business entities rather than for the persons who own or are associated with the business.

Continuity. Unless there is strong evidence to the contrary, it is assumed that the business will continue to operate as a going concern. If it were not to continue, then liquidation values, generally much lower, would apply.

Unit of measure. It is assumed that the most practical unit of measure is money and that changes in investment and income will be measured in money. So far, no better unit of measure has been found.

Time period. An essential function of accounting is to provide information for decision making. To accomplish this, it is necessary to establish accounting periods, or systematic time intervals, so that timely accounting data can be developed.

Historical cost. The properties and services acquired by an enterprise are generally recorded at cost (the cash or its equivalent given to acquire the property or service). The cost is spread over the accounting periods that benefit from the expenditure.

Revenue recognition. Revenue relates to the output of goods and services. In most cases revenue is recognized when goods are delivered or services rendered. In some cases, however, revenue is recognized:

1. During production
2. When production is completed
3. When cash is collected

Matching. In determining the proper periodic income, it is necessary to match related costs and expenses to revenue for the period. The cost of the product sold and all expenses incurred in producing the sale should be matched against the revenue.

Objectivity. Accounting entries should be based on objective evidence to the fullest extent possible. Business documents originating outside the firm provide the best evidence. Estimates should be supported by variable objective data.

Consistency. A standard method of treatment from one year to the next is necessary if periodic financial statements are to be compared with one another. Where a different method will state results and financial position more fairly, the change may be made if the effect on the statements is clearly disclosed.

Full disclosure. Financial statements and notes to financial statements should contain relevant data of a material nature. They should disclose such things as a change in accounting methods.

Materiality. The accountant must be practical and must consider the relative importance of data. The decision as to what is material and what is unimportant requires judgment rather than inflexible rules.

Conservatism. Accountants necessarily make many value judgments that affect financial statements. In these judgments, it is desirable that they provide for all possible losses and not anticipate profits as yet unrealized.

Summary

1. The accounting equation is _____ = _____ + _____.
2. Items owned by a business that have monetary value are _____.
3. _____ is the interest of the owners in a business.
4. Money owed to an outsider is a(n) _____.
5. The difference between assets and liabilities is _____.
6. An investment in the business increases _____ and _____.
7. The statement that shows net income for the period is the _____.

Answers: 1. Assets, liabilities, owner's equity; 2. Assets; 3. Owner's equity; 4. Liability; 5. Owner's equity; 6. Assets, owner's equity; 7. Income statement

Solved Problems

1.1   Compute the amount of the missing element:

	Assets	Liabilities	Owner's Equity
(a)	$24,000	$19,000	?
(b)	$16,500	?	$12,300
(c)	?	$2,700	$14,000
(d)	$15,665	$9,406	?

SOLUTION

(a)	$5,000	($24,000 − $19,000)
(b)	$4,200	($16,500 − $12,300)
(c)	$16,700	($2,700 + $14,000)
(d)	$6,259	($15,665 − $9,406)

1.2   Transactions completed by B. Spencer, M.D., appear below. Indicate increase (+), decrease (−), or no change (0) in the accompanying table.

$$Assets = Liabilities + Owner's\ Equity$$

Paid rent expense for month
Paid weekly salary for assistant
Cash fees collected for the week
Bought equipment, using cash
Bought equipment on account
Paid a creditor money owed

SOLUTION

	Assets	= Liabilities	+ Owner's Equity
Reduction of cash, capital	−	0	−
Reduction of cash, capital	−	0	−
Increase in cash, capital	+	0	+
Increase equipment, reduce cash	+/−	0	0
Increase equipment, A/P	+	+	0
Reduce cash, A/P	−	−	0

1.3 Rocco Burday operates a shoe repair shop known as the Repair Center. The balances of his accounts on June 1 of the current year were as follows:

Cash	$5,400
Supplies	600
Equipment	3,200
Accounts Payable	3,000
Capital	6,200

The transactions during the month of June appear below.
(1)   Paid salaries of $350
(2)   Paid creditors on account $2,000
(3)   Bought additional equipment on account for $3,100
(4)   Received cash from customers for repair service, $3,600
(5)   Paid delivery expense, $140
(6)   Inventory of supplies at end of the month was $275
(7)   Mr. Burday withdrew for his personal use $250

Record the transactions in the form provided.

	Cash	+	Supplies	+	Equipment	=	Accounts Payable	+	R. Burday, Capital
			Assets			=	**Liabilities** +		**Owner's Equity**
Balance, June 1	$5,400		$600		$3,200		$3,000		$6,200
(1)									
Balance									
(2)									
Balance									
(3)									
Balance									
(4)									
Balance									
(5)									
Balance									
(6)									
Balance									
(7)									
Balance, June 30									

SOLUTION

	Cash	+	Supplies	+	Equipment	=	Accounts Payable	+	R. Burday, Capital	
			Assets			=	**Liabilities** +		**Owner's Equity**	
Balance, June 1	$5,400	+	$600	+	$3,200	=	$3,000	+	$6,200	
(1)	−350								−350	Salaries Expense
Balance	$5,050	+	$600	+	$3,200	=	$3,000	+	$5,850	
(2)	−2,000						−2,000			
Balance	$3,050	+	$600	+	$3,200	=	$1,000	+	$5,850	
(3)					+3,100		+3,100			
Balance	$3,050	+	$600	+	$6,300	=	$4,100	+	$5,850	
(4)	+3,600								+3,600	Repair Income
Balance	$6,650	+	$600	+	$6,300	=	$4,100	+	$9,450	
(5)	−140								−140	Delivery Expense
Balance	$6,510	+	$600	+	$6,300	=	$4,100	+	$9,310	
(6)			−325*						−325	Supplies Expense
Balance	$6,510	+	$275	+	$6,300	=	$4,100	+	$8,985	
(7)	−250								−250	Drawing
Balance, June 30	$6,260	+	$275	+	$6,300	=	$4,100	+	$8,735	

---

*$600 (beginning inventory) − $275 (ending inventory) = $325 (amount used, or supplies expense).

1.4 Prepare an income statement based on the following information: Fees Income, $38,000; Supplies Expense, $16,000; Salaries Expense, $12,000; Miscellaneous Expense, $7,000.

SOLUTION

Income Statement		
Fees Income		$38,000
Expenses		
Supplies Expense	$16,000	
Salaries Expense	12,000	
Miscellaneous Expense	7,000	
Total Expenses		35,000
Net Income		$ 3,000

1.5 From the information that follows, prepare a classified balance sheet as of December 31.

Cash	$ 6,000
Accounts Receivable	3,000
Supplies	1,000
Equipment	14,000
Accounts Payable	2,500
Notes Payable	1,500
Mortgage Payable	12,000
Capital, December 31	8,000

SOLUTION

ASSETS		
Current Assets		
Cash	$6,000	
Accounts Receivable	3,000	
Supplies	1,000	
Total Current Assets		$10,000
Fixed Assets		
Equipment		14,000
Total Assets		$24,000
LIABILITIES AND OWNER'S EQUITY		
Current Liabilities		
Notes Payable	$1,500	
Accounts Payable	2,500	
Total Current Liabilities		$ 4,000
Long-Term Liabilities		
Mortgage Payable		12,000
Total Liabilities		$16,000
Capital		8,000
Total Liabilities and Owner's Equity		$24,000

Chapter 2
ANALYZING AND RECORDING TRANSACTIONS

Debits And Credits: The Double-Entry System

A separate account is maintained for each item that appears on the balance sheet (assets, liabilities, and owner's equity) and on the income statement (revenue and expense). Thus, an account may be defined as a *record of the increases, decreases, and balances in an individual item of asset, liability, owner's equity, revenue, or expense.* The simplest form of the account is known as the "T" account because it resembles the letter "T." The account has three parts: (1) the name of the account and the account number, (2) the debit side (left side), and (3) the credit side (right side). When an amount is entered on the left side of an account, it is a *debit* and the account is said to be *debited*. When an amount is entered on the right side, it is a *credit* and the account is said to be *credited*. The abbreviations for debit and credit are Dr. and Cr., respectively. Whether an increase in a given item is credited or debited depends on the category of the item. By convention, asset and expense increases are recorded as debits, and asset and expense decreases are recorded as credits. Liability, capital, and revenue increases are recorded as credits, whereas decreases in these accounts are recorded as debits. The following tables summarize the rule:

Assets and Expenses		Liabilities, Owner's Equity, and Income	
Dr.	Cr.	Dr.	Cr.
+	–	–	+
(Increases)	(Decreases)	(Decreases)	(Increases)

An account has a debit balance when the sum of its debits exceeds the sum of its credits; it has a credit balance when the sum of the credits is the greater. In *double-entry accounting,* which is in almost universal use worldwide, there are equal debit and credit entries for every transaction. When only two accounts are affected, the debit and credit accounts are

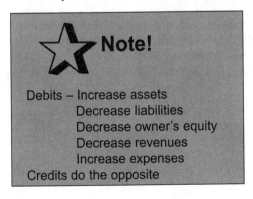

Note!

Debits – Increase assets
Decrease liabilities
Decrease owner's equity
Decrease revenues
Increase expenses
Credits do the opposite

equal. If more than two accounts are affected, the total of the debit entries must equal the total of the credit entries.

The Ledger

The complete set of accounts for a business entity is called a *ledger.* It is the "reference book" of the accounting system and is used to classify and summarize transactions and to prepare data for financial statements. It is also a valuable source of information for managerial purposes, giving, for example, the amount of sales for the period or the cash balance at the end of the period.

The Chart of Accounts

It is desirable to establish a systematic method of identifying and locating each account in the ledger. The *chart of accounts,* sometimes called the *code of accounts,* is a listing of the accounts by title and numerical designation. In some companies the chart of accounts may run to hundreds of items. In designing a numbering structure for the accounts, it is important to provide adequate flexibility to permit expansion without having to revise the basic system. Generally, blocks of numbers are assigned to various groups of accounts, such as assets, liabilities, etc. There are various systems of coding, depending on the needs and desires of the company.

The Trial Balance

Because every transaction results in an equal amount of debits and credits in the ledger, the total of all debit entries in the ledger should equal the total of all credit entries. At the end of the accounting period we check this equality by preparing a schedule called a *trial balance,* which compares the total of all *debit balances* with the total of all *credit balances.* The procedure is as follows:

1. Record the balance of each account, entering debit balances in the debit column and credit balances in the credit column. (Note: Asset and expense accounts are debited for increases

and would normally have debit balances. Liabilities, capital, and income accounts are credited for increases and would normally have credit balances.)
2. Add the columns and record the totals.
3. Compare the totals. They must both be the same.

If the totals agree, the trial balance is in balance, indicating the equality of the debits and credits for the hundreds or thousands of transactions entered in the ledger. Although the trial balance provides *arithmetic* proof of the accuracy of the records, it does not provide *theoretical* proof. For example, if the purchase of equipment was incorrectly debited to Expense, the trial balance columns may agree, but theoretically the accounts would be wrong, as Expense would be overstated and Equipment understated. In addition to providing proof of arithmetic accuracy in accounts, the trial balance facilitates the preparation of the periodic financial statements.

 Important Point!

The trial balance **only** (1) shows that debits and credits balance and (2) facilitates the preparation of financial statements.

The Journal

In the preceding chapters we discussed the nature of business transactions and the manner in which they are analyzed and classified. The primary emphasis was the *why* rather than the *how* of accounting operations; we aimed at an understanding of the *reason* for making the entry in a particular way. We showed the effects of transactions by making entries in T accounts. However, these entries do not provide the necessary data for a particular transaction, nor do they provide a chronological record of transactions. The missing information is furnished by the use of an accounting form known as the journal.

The journal, or day book, is the book of *original* entry for accounting data. Subsequently, the data is transferred or *posted* to the ledger, the book of subsequent or *secondary* entry. The various transactions are evidenced by sales tickets, purchase invoices, check stubs, etc. On the basis of this evidence, the transactions are entered in chronological order in the journal. The process is called *journalizing*.

There are a number of different journals that may be used in a business. For our purposes they may be grouped into (1) the general journal and (2) specialized journals. The latter types, which are used in businesses with a large number of repetitive transactions, are described in Chapter 12. To illustrate journalizing, we here use the general journal, whose standard form is shown below.

General Journal

Date (1)	Description (2)	P.R. (3)	Dr. (4)	Cr. (5)
19X8 Oct.7	Cash	11	10,000	
	John Nennessy, Capital	31		10,000
	Invested cash in business			
	(6)			

Journalizing

We describe the entries in the general journal according to the numbering above.

(1) **Date.** The year, month, and day of the entry are written in the date column. The year and month do not have to be repeated for additional entries until a new month occurs or a new page is needed.

(2) **Description.** The account title to be debited is entered on the first line, next to the date column. The name of the account to be credited is entered on the line below and indented.

(3) **P.R. (Posting Reference).** Nothing is entered in this column until the particular entry is posted, that is, until the amounts are

transferred to the related ledger accounts. The posting process will be described next in the chapter.

(4) *Debit.* The debit amount for each account is entered in this column adjacent to the left margin. Generally there is only one item, but there can be two or more separate items.

(5) *Credit.* The credit amount for each account is indented and entered in this column. Here again, there is generally only one account, but two or more accounts with different amounts can be involved. When there is more than one debit or credit in a single entry, the transaction is known as a compound entry.

(6) *Explanation.* A brief description of the transaction is usually made on the line below the credit. Some accountants feel that if the transaction is obvious, the explanation may be omitted. Generally a blank line is left between the explanation and the next entry.

Posting

The process of transferring information from the journal to the ledger for the purpose of summarizing is called *posting*. Primarily a clerical task, posting is ordinarily carried out in the following steps:

1. *Record the amount and date.* The date and the amounts of the debits and credits are entered in the appropriate accounts.
2. *Record the posting reference in the account.* The number of the journal page is entered in the account.
3. *Record the posting in the journal.* For cross-referencing, the code number of the account is now entered in the P.R. column of the journal.

Summary

1. To classify and summarize a single item of an account group, we use a form called a(n) _____.
2. The accounts make up a record called a(n) _____.
3. The left side of an account is known as the _____, and the right side is the _____.
4. Increases in all asset accounts are _____.

5. Increases in all liability accounts are _____.
6. Increases in all equity (capital) accounts are _____.
7. Increases in all revenue accounts are _____.
8. Increases in all expense accounts are _____.
9. Expenses are debited because they decrease _____.
10. The schedule showing the balance of each account in the general ledger at the end of the period is known as the _____.
11. The initial book for recording all transactions is known as the _____.
12. The process of transferring information from the journal to the ledger is known as _____.
13. The list of code numbers that identifies the entries in the journal is called the _____.
14. The process of recording transactions in the journal is called _____.
15. The complete process of accounting is called the _____.

Answers: 1. Account; 2. Ledger; 3. Debit, credit; 4. Debits; 5. Credits; 6. Credits; 7. Credits; 8. Debits; 9. Owner's equity; 10. Trial balance; 11. Journal; 12. Posting; 13. Chart of accounts; 14. Journalizing; 15. Accounting cycle

Solved Problems

2.1 For each transaction in the table below, indicate the account to be debited and the account to be credited by placing the letter representing the account in the appropriate column.

Name of Account
(a) Accounts Payable
(b) Capital
(c) Cash
(d) Drawing
(e) Equipment
(f) Fees Income
(g) Notes Payable
(h) Rent Expense
(i) Salaries Expense
(j) Supplies
(k) Supplies Expense

Transaction	Dr.	Cr.
1. Invested cash in the firm		
2. Paid rent for month		
3. Received cash fees for services		
4. Paid salaries		
5. Bought equipment on account		
6. Paid 1/2 balance on equipment		
7. Bought supplies on account		
8. Borrowed money from bank, giving a note in exchange		
9. Supplies inventory showed 1/3 used during the month		
10. Withdrew cash for personal use		

	Dr.	Cr.
1.	(c)	(b)
2.	(h)	(c)
3.	(c)	(f)
4.	(i)	(c)
5.	(e)	(a)
6.	(a)	(c)
7.	(j)	(a)
8	(c)	(g)
9.	(k)	(j)
10.	(d)	(c)

2.2 For the transactions below, record each entry in a T account.

(1) The Nu-Look Dry Cleaning Company opened a business bank account by depositing $12,000 on November 1.

(2) Purchased supplies with cash, $220.

(3) Purchased dry cleaning equipment from Hill Cleaning Equipment, Inc., for $3,500, paying $1,500 in cash with the balance on account.

(4) Paid rent for the month, $825.

(5) Cash sales for the month totaled $1,850.

(6) Paid salaries of $375.

(7) Paid $500 on account to Hill Cleaning Equipment, Inc.

(8) The cost of supplies used was determined to be $60.

SOLUTION

Cash			11		Equipment		13			Cleaning Income	41
(1)	12,000	220	(2)	(3)	3,500					1,850	(5)
(5)	1,850	1,500	(3)								
10,430	13,850	825	(4)		Accounts Payable		21			Rent Expense	51
		375	(6)								
		500	(7)	(7)	500	2,000	(3)	(4)	825		
		3,420				1,500					
										Salaries Expense	52
	Supplies		12		Capital		31	(6)	375		
(2)	220	60	(8)			12,000	(1)				
	160									Supplies Expense	53
								(8)	60		

2.3 Prepare a trial balance as of November 30 for the Nu-Look Dry Cleaning Company, using the account balances in Prob. 2.2.

SOLUTION

Nu-Look Dry Cleaning Company		
Trial Balance		
November 30, 19X8		
	Debit	Credit
Cash	$10,830	
Supplies	160	
Equipment	3,500	
Accounts Payable		$ 1,500
Nu-Look Dry Cleaning Company, Capital		12,000
Cleaning Income		1,850
Rent Expense	425	
Salaries Expense	375	
Supplies Expense	60	
	$15,350	$15,350

2.4 Record the following entries in the general journal for the Sylvia Cleaning Company.

(1) Invested $12,000 cash in the business.
(2) Paid $1,000 for office furniture.
(3) Bought equipment costing $8,000 on account.

(4) Received $2,200 in cleaning income.
(5) Paid one-fifth of the amount owed on the equipment.

SOLUTION

	Debit	Credit
(1) Cash	12,000	
Sylvia, capital		12,000
(2) Office furniture	1,000	
Cash		1,000
(3) Equipment	8,000	
Accounts Payable		8,000
(4) Cash	2,200	
Cleaning Income		2,200
(5) Accounts Payable	1,600	
Cash		1,600

2.5 Listed below are the January transactions for Big Ben Clock Repair Store, owned by David McDonald. Record them in general journal form.

Jan. 1 Invested $7,000 cash and equipment with a book value of $2,800
3 Paid first month's rent, $700
5 Cash repairs, $1,400
7 Purchased supplies on account, $325
8 Repaired a grandfather clock on account, $900
8 Paid wages, $275
11 Purchased equipment, $550 cash
12 Cash repairs, $2,700
15 Purchased equipment on account, $400
17 Paid for advertising, $325
19 Withdrew $500 for personal expenses
21 Received $500 on account from Jan. 8 transaction
22 Paid wages, $325
25 Cash repairs, $3,400
26 Paid $400 on account from Jan. 15 transaction
29 Repaired a clock on account, $345

SOLUTION

General Journal

Date		Debit	Credit
Jan. 1	Cash	7,000	
	Equipment	2,800	
	David McDonald, Capital		9,800
3	Rent Expense	700	
	Cash		700
5	Cash	1,400	
	Repair Income		1,400
7	Supplies	325	
	Accounts Payable		325
8	Accounts receivable	900	
	Repair Income		900
8	Wage Expense	275	
	Cash		275
11	Equipment	550	
	Cash		550
12	Cash	2,700	
	Repair Income		2,700
15	Equipment	400	
	Accounts Payable		400
17	Advertising Expense	325	
	Cash		325
19	David McDonald, Drawing	500	
	Cash		500
21	Cash	500	
	Accounts Receivable		500
22	Wage Expense	325	
	Cash		325
25	Cash	3,400	
	Repair Income		3,400
26	Accounts Payable	400	
	Cash		400
29	Accounts Receivable	345	
	Repair Income		345

Chapter 3
ADJUSTING AND CLOSING PROCEDURES

IN THIS CHAPTER:

✔ *The Accrual Basis of Accounting*
✔ *Adjusting Entries*
✔ *Closing Entries*
✔ *Reversing Entries*
✔ *Summary*
✔ *Solved Problems*

The Accrual Basis of Accounting

As mentioned earlier, accounting records are kept on the *accrual* basis, except in the case of very small businesses. This means that *revenue is recognized when earned, regardless of when cash is actually collected, and expense is matched to the revenue, regardless of when cash is paid out.* Most revenue is earned when goods or services are delivered. At this time, title to the goods or services is transferred and a legal obligation to pay for such goods or services is created. Some

revenue, such as rental income, is recognized on a time basis, and is earned when the specified period of time has passed. The accrual concept demands that expenses be kept in step with revenue, so that each month sees only that month's expenses applied against the revenue for that month. The necessary matching is brought about through a type of journal entry. In this chapter we shall discuss these *adjusting entries*, and also the *closing entries* through which the adjusted balances are ultimately transferred to balance sheet accounts at the end of the fiscal year.

Adjusting Entries

To adjust expense or income items that have already been recorded, a reclassification is required; that is, amounts have to be transferred from an asset, one of the prepaid expense accounts (e.g., Prepaid Insurance), to an expense account (Insurance Expense). The following five examples will show how adjusting entries are made for the principal types of *recorded expenses*.

1. Prepaid Insurance

Assume that on April 1, a business paid a $1,200 premium for one year's insurance in advance. This represents an increase in one asset (prepaid expense) and a decrease in another asset (cash). Thus the entry would be

April 1	Prepaid Insurance	1,200
	Cash	1,200

At the end of April, one-twelfth of the $1,200, or $100, has expired. Therefore, an adjustment has to be made, decreasing or crediting Prepaid Insurance and increasing or debiting Insurance Expense. The entry would be

April 1	Insurance Expense	100
	Prepaid Insurance	100

Thus, $100 would be shown as Insurance Expense in the income statement for April and the balance of $1,100 would be shown as part of Prepaid Insurance in the balance sheet.

2. Prepaid Rent

Assume that on April 1 a business paid $1,800 to cover the rent for the next three months. The full amount would have been recorded as a prepaid expense in April. Since there is a three-month period involved, the rent expense each month is $600. The balance of Prepaid Rent would be $1,200 at the beginning of May. The adjusting entry for April would be

Rent Expense	600	
Prepaid Rent		600

3. Supplies

A type of prepayment that is somewhat different from those previously described is the payment for office supplies or factory supplies. Assume that on April 1, $400 worth of supplies were purchased. There were none on hand before. This would increase the asset Supplies and decrease the asset Cash. At the end of April, when expense and revenue are to be matched and statements prepared, a count of the supplies on hand will be made. Assume that the inventory count shows that $250 of supplies are still on hand. Then the amount consumed during April was $150. The two entries are as follows:

April 1	Supplies	400	
	Cash		400
30	Supplies Expense	150	
	Supplies		150

Supplies Expense of $150 will be included in the April income statement; Supplies of $250 will be included as an asset on the balance sheet of April 30.

4. Accumulated Depreciation

In the previous three adjusting entries, the balances of the assets mentioned were all reduced. These assets usually lose their value in a relatively short period of time. However, assets that have a longer life expectancy (such as a building) are treated differently because the accounting profession wants to keep a balance sheet record of the equipment's original, or historical, cost. Thus, the adjusting entry needed to reflect the true value of the long-term asset each year must allocate its original cost, known as depreciation. In order to accomplish the objectives of keeping original cost of the equipment and also maintaining a running total of the depreciation allocated, we must create a new account entitled Accumulated Depreciation. This account, known as a contra asset (an asset that has the opposite balance to its asset), summarizes and accumulates the amount of depreciation over the equipment's total useful life. Assume that machinery costing $15,000 was purchased on February 1 of the current year and was expected to last ten years. With the straight line method of depreciation (equal charges each period), the depreciation would be $1,500 a year, or $125 a month. The adjusting entry would be as follows:

Depreciation Expense	125	
Accumulated Depreciation		125

At the end of April, Accumulated Depreciation would have a balance of $375, representing three months' accumulated depreciation. The account would be shown in the balance sheet as follows:

Machinery	$15,000	
Less: Accumulated Depreciation	375	$14,625

5. Unearned Rent

In the following example, a new type of account is introduced. Known as Unearned Rent, this account is a liability and represents income that was received before the service was completed. In other words, the income was not earned. After a period of time, when the income is actually earned, an adjusting entry is made to reduce the liability account, and the earned income account is then recorded.

Assume that a landlord received $1,800 rent in advance on April 1. The following entry would be made (considering $600/month for rent):

| April 1 | Cash | 1,800 | |
| | Unearned Rent | | 1,800 |

At the end of April, one month's rent has been earned and Unearned Rent would be debited:

| April 30 | Unearned Rent | 600 | |
| | Rent Income | | 600 |

6. Covering Unrecorded Data

In the previous section we discussed various kinds of adjustments to accounts to which entries had already been made. Now we consider those instances in which an expense has been incurred or an income earned but the applicable amount has not been recorded during the month. For example, if salaries are paid on a weekly basis, the last week of the month may run into the next month. If April ends on a Tuesday, then the first two days of the week will apply to April and will be an April expense, whereas the last three days will be a May expense.

To arrive at the proper total for salaries for the month of April, we must include, along with the April payrolls that were paid in April, the two days' salary that was not paid until May. Thus, we make an entry to accrue the two days' salary.

7. Accrued Salaries

Assume that April 30 falls on Tuesday. Then, two days of that week will apply to April and three days to May. The payroll is $500 per day, $2,500 per week. For this example, $1,000 would thus apply to April and $1,500 to May. The entry would be as follows:

| April 30 | Salaries Expense | 1,000 | |
| | Salaries Payable | | 1,000 |

When the payment of the payroll is made—on May 8—the entry would be as follows:

May 8	Salaries Expense	1,500	
	Salaries Payable	1,000	
	Cash		2,500

As can be seen above, $1,000 was charged to expense in April and $1,500 in May. The debit to Accrued Salaries Payable of $1,000 in May merely canceled the credit entry made in April, when the liability was set up for the April salaries expense.

Remember

Adjusting entries are necessary to comply with the **accrual basis** of accounting. Each adjusting entry updates accounts to the end of the accounting period.

Closing Entries

The information for the month-to-month adjusting entries and the related financial statements can be obtained from the work sheet, whose use will be fully described in a later chapter. After the income statement and balance sheet have been prepared from the work sheet for the last month in the fiscal year, a summary account—known as Income Summary—is set up. Then, by means of *closing entries*, each income account is debited so as to produce a zero balance, and the total amount for the closed-out accounts is credited to Income Summary. Similarly, the individual expense accounts are closed out by crediting them, and their total amount is debited to the summary account. Thus, the new fiscal year starts with zero balances in the income and expense accounts, whereas the Income Summary balance gives the net income or the net loss for the old year.

To illustrate the closing procedure, the following example is given:

Alan Bagon, Lawyer
Trial Balance
April 30, 19X8

Cash	$4,700	
Supplies	100	
Equipment	2,500	
Accounts Payable		$1,500
Alan Bagon, Capital		5,000
Alan Bagon, Drawing	300	
Fees Income		2,000
Rent Expense	500	
Salaries Expense	200	
Supplies Expense	200	
	$8,500	$8,500

The closing entries are as follows:

1. **Close out revenue accounts.** Debit the individual revenue accounts and credit their total to Income Summary.

April 30	Fees Income	2,000	
	Income Summary		2,000

2. **Close out expense accounts.** Credit the individual expense accounts and debit their total to Income Summary.

April 30	Income Summary	900	
	Rent Expense		500
	Salaries Expense		200
	Supplies Expense		200

3. **Close out the Income Summary account.** If there is a profit, the credit made for total income in (1) above will exceed the debit made for total expense in (2) above. Therefore to close out the balance to zero, a debit entry will be made to Income Summary. A credit will be made to the Capital account to transfer the net income for the period. If expenses exceed income, then a loss had been sustained and a credit will be made to Income Summary and a debit to the Capital account. The entry for the example above is:

April 30	Income Summary	1,100	
	Capital Account		1,100

4. **Close out the drawing account.** The Drawing Account is credited for the total amount of the drawings for the period, and the Capital account is debited for that amount. The difference between net income and drawing for the period represents the net change in the Capital account for the period. The net income of $1,100 less drawings of $300 results in a net increase of $800 in the Capital account. The closing entry is as follows:

April 30	Capital Account	300	
	Drawing Account		300

Note!

Closing entries:
1 Reset revenue and expense account balances to zero to begin the next period
2 Move the period's net income or loss to owner's equity
3 Revise owner's equity for the effect of owner withdrawals

Reversing Entries

The *reversing entry* (which is optional) is an accounting method that reverses a specific adjusting entry that was made at the end of the previous period. Not all adjusting entries need to be reversed. The reversing entry is made at the beginning of a period and, as a result, transactions for the remainder of the current year are routine. The amounts used in the reversing entry are identical to those used in the adjusting entry. The rule to determine whether or not to reverse is as follows: "Any adjusting entry that creates an asset or liability has to be reversed."

Assume that Judy Jones receives $500 weekly ($100 daily) salary and that the last Friday in December falls on December 27. The entry to record the salary for the week ending Friday, December 27, would be

Salary Expense	500	
Cash		500

However, on December 31, the accrual of Salaries Payable must be made for Monday and Tuesday, December 30 and 31.

Salary Expense	200	
Salaries Payable		200

Since Salaries Payable is a liability and was created by an adjusting entry, a reversing entry would be needed at the beginning of January of the following year.

Salaries Payable	200	
Salary Expense		200

Now when the salaries are paid on the first Friday in January, the usual journal entry may be made, which will result in the correct allocation of the $500 between December and January.

Salary Expense	500	
Cash		500

Please note that not all business entities choose to use reversing entries.

Computerized Systems

In order to make them more reliable and to facilitate the preparation of the various financial statements and other reports, many accounting systems are now computerized. Computerized systems also facilitate the use of special journals, as discussed in Chapter 12.

Whether a system is computerized or manual, however, the basic components remain the same. Transactions must be journalized and posted. Adjusting entries must be entered, and financial statements must be prepared. Indeed, a computerized system is merely a faster, and perhaps easier, version of a manual system. Because it is imperative that students of accounting understand the basic components of an accounting system, whether computerized or manual, in this text, our discussions focus on manual systems.

The key elements of a computerized system are hardware, software, and personnel. Each of these elements can be designed to fit the specific needs and environment of the entity.

You Need to Know

The Accounting Cycle
  Analyze
  Journalize
  Post
  Trial balance
  Adjusting entries
  Adjusted trial balance
  Prepare financial statements
  Closing entries
  Post-closing trial balance
  Reversing entries

Summary

1. The basis of accounting that recognizes revenue when earned, regardless of when the cash is received, and matches expenses to the revenues, regardless of when cash is paid out, is known as _____.

2. An adjusting entry that records the expired amount of prepaid insurance would debit the _____ account.

3. Supplies on hand are classified as a(n) _____ and appear in the _____, whereas supplies used during the period are a(n) _____ and appear in the _____.

4. Accumulated Depreciation appears in the balance sheet as a(n) _____ from the related asset.

5. Accrued Salaries are treated in the balance sheet as a(n) _____, whereas salaries actually incurred appear in the income statement as a(n) _____.

6. Income that has been earned but not yet received is known as _____.

7. Expenses that have been incurred but not yet paid are known as _____.

8. Revenue and expense accounts are closed to a summary account known as _____.

9. For a sole proprietorship, all income, expense, drawing, and summary accounts will be netted and closed ultimately to the _____ account.

10. A trial balance taken after closing entries (post-closing trial balance) will involve only _____,_____, and _____ accounts.

Answers: 1. Accrual basis; 2. Insurance Expense; 3. Asset, balance sheet, expense, income statement; 4. Deduction; 5. Liability, expense; 6. Unrecorded revenue or accrued income; 7. Accrued expenses; 8. Income Summary; 9. Capital; 10. Asset, Liability, Capital

Solved Problems

3.1 On January 1, 19X9, Hill Top Farm purchased a 3-year fire insurance policy for $3,600, paying cash. The entry made on January 1, 19X9, was a debit to Prepaid Insurance and a credit to Cash. What is the year-end adjusting entry?

SOLUTION

Insurance Expense	1,200*	
Prepaid Insurance		1,200

*$3,600 x 1/3 = $1,200

3.2 Hill Top Apartments rented an apartment on November 1, 19X9, for 6 months, receiving $3,000 in advance. The entry made on November 1 was

| Cash | 3,000 | |
| Rental Income | | 3,000 |

What would the year-end adjusting entry be?

SOLUTION

| Rental Income | 2,000 | |
| Unearned Rent | | 2,000 |

3.3 The business received $6,000 as an advance payment for work to be done for a customer. At the end of the year, $4,000 of the services had been performed. (a) Prepare the adjusting entry if the original amount had been credited to Unearned Income. (b) What type of account is Unearned Income?

SOLUTION

(a)	Unearned Income	4,000	
	Service Income		4,000
(b)	It is unrealized income and therefore a liability.		

3.4 A business pays weekly salaries of $10,000 on Friday for a 5-day week. Show the adjusting entry when the fiscal period ends on (a) Tuesday; (b) Thursday.

SOLUTION

(a)	Salaries Expense	4,000	
	Salaries Payable		4,000
(b)	Salaries Expense	8,000	
	Salaries Payable		8,000

3.5 Based on the balances below, prepare entries to close out (a) revenue accounts, (b) expense accounts, (c) the Income Summary account, (d) the Drawing account.

P. Silver, Capital		$22,000
P. Silver, Drawing	$6,000	
Service Income		12,000
Interest Income		1,500
Salaries Expense	8,000	
Rent Expense	4,000	
Depreciation Expense	3,000	
Interest Expense	2,000	

SOLUTION

(a)	Service Income	12,000	
	Interest Income	1,500	
	Income Summary		13,500
(b)	Income Summary	17,000	
	Salaries Expense		8,000
	Rent Expense		4,000
	Depreciation Expense		3,000
	Interest Expense		2,000
(c)	P. Silver, Capital	3,500*	
	Income Summary		3,500
(d)	P. Silver, Capital	6,000	
	P. Silver, Drawing		6,000

*3,500 represents a net loss and is debited to the Capital account.

Chapter 4
SUMMARIZING AND REPORTING VIA THE WORK SHEET

IN THIS CHAPTER:

✔ *The Work Sheet*
✔ *Work Sheet Procedures for a Service Business*
✔ *Work Sheet Procedures for a Merchandising Business*
✔ *Inventory and Purchases Treatment*
✔ *Cost of Goods Sold*
✔ *The Classified Income Statement*
✔ *The Merchandising Work Sheet*
✔ *Summary*
✔ *Solved Problems*

The Work Sheet

The recording of transactions and the adjusting and closing procedures have been discussed in previous chapters. It is reasonable to expect that among the hundreds of computations and clerical tasks involved some errors will occur, such as posting a debit as a credit. One of the best ways to avoid errors in the permanent accounting records, and also simplify the work at the end of the period, is to make use of an informal record called the work sheet.

The work sheet is usually prepared in pencil on a large sheet called analysis paper. Here, the ledger accounts are adjusted, balanced, and arranged in proper form for preparing the financial statements. All procedures can be reviewed quickly, and the adjusting and closing entries can be made in the formal records with less chance of error. Moreover, with the data for the income statement and balance sheet already proved out on the work sheet, these statements can be prepared more quickly.

Work Sheet Procedures
for a Service Business

A typical service business will suppose the work sheet to have eight monetary columns, both a debit and credit column for each of the four groups of figures: trial balance, adjustments, income statement, and balance sheet. A ten-column work sheet also is used which places a column in the middle, which is used for the adjusted trial balance, merely combining the first two columns. The steps for completing the work sheet are:

1.   Enter the trial balance figures from the ledger.
2.   Enter the adjustments.
3.   Extend the adjusted figures to either the income statement or balance sheet columns.
4.   Total the income statement columns and the balance sheet columns.
5.   Enter the net income or net loss.

Below is an example of a worksheet for the Thomas Company for the
year ended 19X8. Recognize how the debit and credit columns balance
for each different group of figures.

Thomas Company
Work Sheet
Year Ended December 31, 19X8

Account Title	Trial Balance Debit	Trial Balance Credit	Adjustments Debit	Adjustments Credit	Income Statement Debit	Income Statement Credit	Balance Sheet Debit	Balance Sheet Credit
Cash	3,510						3,510	
Accounts Receivable	4,010						4,010	
Supplies	1,050			(a) 500			550	
Prepaid Rent	400			(b) 100			300	
Equipment	18,000						18,000	
Accumulated Deprec.		3,000		(c) 1,800				4,800
Notes Payable		4,000						4,000
Accounts Payable		2,380						2,380
Taxes Payable		400						400
Jane Thomas, Capital		13,690						13,690
Jane Thomas, Drawing	2,000						2,000	
Service Fees Income		10,500				10,500		
Salaries Expense	4,600		(d) 200		4,800			
Misc. Expense	400				400			
	33,970	33,970						
Supplies Expense			(a) 500		500			
Rent Expense			(b) 100		100			
Depreciation Expense			(c) 1,800		1,800			
Salaries Payable				(d) 200				200
Interest Expense			(e) 40		40			
Interest Payable				(e) 40				40
			2,640	2,640	7,640	10,500	28,370	25,510
Net Income					2,860			2,860
					10,500	10,500	28,370	28,370

Work Sheet Procedures for a Merchandising Business

Merchandising businesses are those whose income derives largely from
buying or selling goods rather than from rendering services. The work
sheet for a merchandising business will carry new accounts and head-
ings such as Inventory, Cost of Goods Sold, and Purchases. First, we
will discuss these individual new accounts and then illustrate their inter-
relation on the work sheet.

Inventory and Purchases Treatment

Inventory represents the value of the goods on hand at either the beginning or the end of the accounting period. The beginning balance would be the same amount as the ending balance from the previous period. Generally, not all merchandise purchased is sold in the same period; so unsold merchandise must be counted and priced, and the total recorded in the ledger as Ending Inventory. The amount of this inventory will be shown as an asset in the balance sheet. The dollar amount of goods sold during the period will be shown as a classified heading known as Cost of Goods Sold in the income statement.

Example 4.1

Assume that the January 1 (beginning) inventory is $20,000 and the December 31 (ending) inventory is $26,000. Two adjusting entries are required to show the replacement of the old by the new inventory:

Entry 1   Income Summary   20,000*
                      Merchandise Inventory   20,000

*The $20,000 balance in the Inventory account that appears in the trial balance represents the beginning balance, whose amount will be transferred to Income Summary.

Entry 2   Merchandise Inventory   26,000*
                      Income Summary   26,000

*The ending inventory of $26,000, is an asset and will be adjusted on the work sheet.

Unlike the procedure for other accounts, both the debit and the credit amounts for Income Summary are extended to the income statement. This is done because the amounts of the debit adjustment and of the credit adjustment are needed to prepare the income statement. It would not be practical to net the two items, as the single figure would not give enough information regarding the beginning and ending inventories. The ending inventory of $26,000 is extended to the debit column of the balance sheet as an asset.

Purchases

It is preferable for managerial purposes to maintain a separate account for purchases rather than including them in the inventory account. This account includes only merchandise purchased for retail and appears in the income statement; purchases of machinery, trucks, etc., to be used in the business are debited to a particular fixed asset account.

The journal entry to record a purchase is as follows:

Purchases	7,000	
Accounts Payable (or Cash)		7,000

At the end of the period, the total in the Purchases account is closed to the Income Summary account.

Transportation-In

The cost of transporting the merchandise, such as freight or trucking, is referred to as transportation-in and is part of the cost of merchandise. Where the purchaser pays the transportation-in, a separate account should be maintained. The entry is as follows:

Transportation-In	1,000	
Accounts Payable (or Cash)		1,000

Purchase Returns

Sometimes goods may be found to be unsatisfactory. The entire shipment may be returned to the vendor, or the vendor may allow a reduction in price without the return of the goods. A return of $600 of goods to the vendor is shown as:

Accounts Payable	600	
Purchase Returns		600

Cost of Goods Sold

Since we do not reflect purchases or sales of goods in the inventory account during the year, we must determine the cost of the inventory remaining on hand at the end of the accounting period and make any adjustments necessary. Ending inventory, or merchandise that has not been sold and is on hand at the end of the period, is an asset that appears on the balance sheet. Cost of Goods Sold appears in the income statement as a deduction from Sales. This cost may be calculated by the following procedure:

Beginning Inventory
+ Net Purchases*
Goods Available for Sale
– Ending Inventory
Cost of Goods Sold

*Net purchases = purchases – purchase returns + transportation-in.

The Classified Income Statement

The classified income statement sets out the amount of each function and enables management, stockholders, analysts, and others to study the changes in function costs over successive accounting periods. There are four functional classifications of the income statement:

1. **Revenue.** This includes gross income from the sale of products or services. It may be designated as Sales, Income from Fees, etc., to indicate gross income, and the gross amount is reduced by Sales Returns and by Sales Discounts to arrive at Net Sales.

2. **Cost of Goods Sold.** Includes the costs related to the products or services sold. It would be relatively simple to compute for a firm that retails furniture; it would be more complex for a manufacturing firm that changes raw materials into finished products.

3. **Operating Expenses.** This includes all expenses or resources consumed in obtaining revenue. Operating expenses can be divided into two groups, *selling expenses* and *general and administrative expenses*. Selling expenses are related to the promotion and sale of the company's products. General and administrative expenses are those related to the overall activities of the business, such as the president's salary.

4. **Other Expenses (net).** Include nonoperating and incidental expenses and/or incomes, such as interest expense or interest income, and are offset against one another and a net amount shown.

J. Ales
Classified Income Statement

(*a*) Gross Sales

Sales of Goods or Services		$25,000	
Less: Sales Returns	$1,250		
Sales Discounts	750	2,000	
Net Sales			$23,000

(*b*) Cost of Goods Sold

Inventory, January 1	$ 2,500	
Purchases	16,500	
Goods Available for Sale	$19,000	
Inventory, December 31	3,000	
Cost of Goods Sold		16,000

(*c*) Gross Profit

Gross Profit	$ 7,000

(*d*) Operating Expenses

Selling Expenses			
Sales Salaries Expense	$1,200		
Travel Expense	200		
Advertising Expense	600	$ 2,000	
General Expenses			
Officers' Salaries Expense	$1,000		
Insurance Expense	600	1,600	
Total Operating Expenses			3,600

(e) Operating Income

      Net Income from Operations $ 3,400

(f) Other Expenses (net)

Interest Expense	$ 500	
Less: Interest Income	100	
Other Expenses (net)		400

(g) Net Income

      Net Income $ 3,000

In this form of income statement, a number of subcategories of cost and expense are used. The key items are labeled with letters, which we will describe briefly.

(a) This is the total of all charges to customers for merchandise sold, both for cash and on account.

(b) This is one of the most important sections of the income statement. It shows the cost of the goods delivered to customers during the period and the relationship of this cost to sales. This relationship can be conveniently compared with the figures for other periods.

(c) The amount of gross profit must be sufficient to pay all the expenses and to yield a reasonable return or profit. The gross profit ratio is a key control figure in managing a business. The selling price must be kept in such a relationship to cost as to yield a desired gross profit. To improve the ratio, sales prices may be increased or costs decreased.

(d) These are the expenses necessary for carrying on the operations of the business. They do not include unusual expenses or financial expenses not of an operating nature, which are classed separately.

(e) This is the amount by which the gross profit exceeds total operating expenses. It measures the degree of profitability from operations, before nonoperating items are considered.

(*f*) This nonoperating item is offset and the net amount is shown in the summary column of the income statement.

(*g*) This represents the net income for the period. Had there been more expenses than income, the figure would be known as *net loss*.

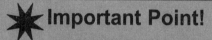

Important Point!

Beginning Inventory +
Net Purchases
Goods Available for Sale −
Ending Inventory
Cost of Goods Sold

The Merchandising Work Sheet

Below is an example of a merchandising work sheet. Notice that it is similar to the service business work sheet, but accounts specific to the merchandising business are included, for example Merchandise Inventory.

Thomas Company
Work Sheet
Year Ended December 31, 19X8

Account Title	Trial Balance Dr.	Trial Balance Cr.	Adjustments Dr.	Adjustments Cr.	Income Statement Dr.	Income Statement Cr.	Balance Sheet Dr.	Balance Sheet Cr.
Cash	3,510						3,510	
Accounts Receivable	4,010						4,010	
Merchandise Inventory	**20,000**		(*a*) **26,000**	(*a*) **20,000**			**26,000**	
Supplies	1,050			(*b*) 500			550	
Prepaid Rent	400			(*c*) 100			300	
Equipment	18,000						18,000	
Accumulated Deprec.		3,000		(*d*) 1,800				4,800
Notes Payable		4,000						4,000
Accounts Payable		2,380						2,380
Taxes Payable		400						400
Jane Thomas, Capital		38,690						38,690
Jane Thomas, Drawing	2,000						2,000	
Sales		30,500				30,500		
Purchases	**25,000**				**25,000**			
Salaries Expense	4,600		(*e*) 200		4,800			
Misc. Expense	400				400			
	78,970	78,970						
Income Summary			(*a*) **20,000**	(*a*) **26,000**	**20,000**	**26,000**		
Supplies Expense			(*b*) 500		500			
Rent Expense			(*c*) 100		100			
Depreciation Expense			(*d*) 1,800		1,800			
Salaries Payable				(*e*) 200				200
Interest Expense			(*f*) 40					
Interest Payable				(*f*) 40	40			40
			48,640	48,640	52,640	56,500	54,370	50,510
Net Income					3,860			3,860
					56,500	56,500	54,370	54,370

Based on the work sheet above, the Cost of Goods Sold section of the income statement would appear as

Cost of Goods Sold	
Inventory (beginning)	$20,000
Purchases	25,000
Goods Available for Sale	$45,000
Less: Inventory (ending)	26,000
Total Cost of Goods Sold	**$19,000**

Remember

Steps in preparing the work sheet:

1. Trial balance
2. Adjustments
3. Extend to financial statement columns
4. Total financial statement columns
5. Enter net income or loss

Summary

1. One of the best accounting methods for avoiding errors in the permanent accounting records and also for simplifying the work at the end of the period is to make use of the _____.
2. On the worksheet, the ledger accounts are _____, _____, and _____ in proper form for preparing financial statements.
3. The balances in the first two columns in the worksheet are obtained from the _____.
4. If the total of the debit column of the income statement in the worksheet is larger than the total of the credit column, the balance is said to be a(n) _____.

Answers: 1. Worksheet; 2. Adjusted, balanced, arranged; 3. Ledger; 4. Net loss

Solved Problems

4.1 Based on the following information, complete the work sheet below.

(a)   Rent expired, $2,100
(b)   Insurance expired, $700
(c)   Supplies on hand, December 31, $300
(d)   Depreciation on equipment, $900
(e)   Salaries accrued, $100

Perez Company
Work Sheet
Year Ended December 31, 19X8

Account Title	Trial Balance Dr.	Trial Balance Cr.	Adjustments Dr.	Adjustments Cr.	Income Statement Dr.	Income Statement Cr.	Balance Sheet Dr.	Balance Sheet Cr.
Cash	12,000							
Accounts Receivable	11,300							
Prepaid Rent	3,100							
Prepaid Insurance	1,600							
Supplies	800							
Equipment	11,500							
Accumulated Deprec.		900						
Accounts Payable		6,400						
J. Perez, Capital		15,200						
J. Perez, Drawing	8,000							
Fees Income		42,500						
Salaries Expense	14,000							
Misc. Expense	2,700							
	65,000	65,000						
Rent Expense								
Insurance Expense								
Supplies Expense								
Depreciation Expense								
Salaries Payable								

SOLUTION

Perez Company
Work Sheet
Year Ended December 31, 19X8

Account Title	Trial Balance Dr.	Trial Balance Cr.	Adjustments Dr.	Adjustments Cr.	Income Statement Dr.	Income Statement Cr.	Balance Sheet Dr.	Balance Sheet Cr.
Cash	12,000						12,000	
Accounts Receivable	11,300						11,300	
Prepaid Rent	3,100			(a) 2,100			1,000	
Prepaid Insurance	1,600			(b) 700			900	
Supplies	800			(c) 500			300	
Equipment	11,500						11,500	
Accumulated Deprec.		900		(d) 900				1,800
Accounts Payable		6,400						6,400
J. Perez, Capital		15,200						15,200
J. Perez, Drawing	8,000						8,000	
Fees Income		42,500				42,500		
Salaries Expense	14,400		(e) 100		14,100			
Misc. Expense	2,700				2,700			
	65,000	65,000						

Account Title	Trial Balance Dr.	Trial Balance Cr.	Adjustments Dr.	Adjustments Cr.	Income Statement Dr.	Income Statement Cr.	Balance Sheet Dr.	Balance Sheet Cr.
Rent Expense			(a) 2,100		2,100			
Insurance Expense			(b) 700		700			
Supplies Expense			(c) 500		500			
Depreciation Expense			(d) 900		900			
Salaries Payable				(e) 100				100
			4,300	4,300	21,000	42,500	45,000	23,500
Net Income					21,500			21,500
					42,500	42,500	45,000	45,000

4.2 Based on the work sheet's income statement columns below, prepare an income statement.

Income Summary	26,400	28,200
Sales		62,500
Purchases	31,400	
Rent Expense	6,000	
Salaries Expense	18,300	
Depreciation Expense	500	
	82,600	90,700

SOLUTION

Sales		$62,500
Cost of Goods Sold		
Merchandise Inventory (beginning)	$26,400	
Purchases	31,400	
Goods Available for Sale	$57,800	
Merchandise Inventory (ending)	28,200	
Cost of Goods Sold		29,600
Gross Profit		$32,900
Operating Expenses		
Rent Expense	$ 6,000	
Salaries Expense	18,300	
Depreciation Expense	500	
Total Expenses		24,800
Net Income		$ 8,100

Chapter 5
INVENTORY VALUATION METHODS

IN THIS CHAPTER:

✔ *Periodic and Perpetual Methods*
✔ *Determining Inventory*
✔ *Inventory Measurement*
✔ *Costing Inventory: FIFO*
✔ *Costing Inventory: LIFO*
✔ *Costing Inventory:*
  Weighted Average
✔ *Comparison of Inventory Methods*
✔ *Specific Identification*
✔ *Summary*
✔ *Solved Problems*

Periodic and Perpetual Methods

Under the *periodic method*, inventory is physically counted at regular intervals. When this system is used, credits are made to the Inventory account or to Purchases not as each sale is made, but rather in total at the end of the accounting period.

The *perpetual method* is generally used when units are of relatively high value and few in number. Running balances by unit and by cost are maintained for units purchased and sold. Individual receipts of goods are debited to the Inventory account, and individual sales are credited to this account. At the end of the accounting period, the costs of goods sold can be determined by adding the costs of the individual items sold.

Example 5.1

If goods were purchased for $10,000 under the periodic system, the Purchases account would be debited. However, under the perpetual system, everything would be debited to Merchandise Inventory. Conversely, every time a sale is made, the account is credited.

Example 5.2

If goods costing $6,000 were sold for $10,000, under the periodic system Sales Income would be credited for the sale of $10,000.

Accounts Receivable	10,000	
Sales Income		10,000

However, under the perpetual system, even though the sale is recognized and treated in the same manner, a second entry is required to show the reduction in the value of Merchandise Inventory.

Accounts Receivable	10,000	
Sales Income		10,000
Cost of Goods Sold	6,000	
Merchandise Inventory		6,000

Thus, the inventory account shows a running balance that always reflects the amount on hand.

Since all inventory transactions under the perpetual inventory system are charged to Merchandise Inventory, any purchase returns or freight charges would not be recognized as separate accounts, but would also fall under the Merchandise Inventory account. Thus, the Purchases, Freight-In, and Purchases Returns accounts are nonexistent under the perpetual system.

Because of the increasing use of bar codes, the perpetual inventory system should eliminate the need to physically count each item in the inventory at the end of every period as in the periodic method. However, most companies continue to take a physical inventory at the end of the year in case of theft, spoilage, or clerical error. Therefore, because of this double-checking, the periodic system is generally used.

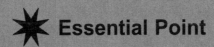

Essential Point

Periodic System—Inventory and cost of goods sold are determined only at end of period

Perpetual System—Inventory and cost of goods sold are determined at the time of each sale

Determining Inventory

Firms that use the periodic system do not keep records that show a continuous count for each product. Rather, the amounts are determined through a physical inventory. A physical inventory is the process of actually counting each item, and documenting totals for individual inventory items.

Goods in Transit

Any goods in transit that have been ordered by the firm should be included in the inventory if the title to the goods has already passed, even if the items are not physically on the premises for the physical count. The term FOB (Free on Board) is used to show the passing of title from the seller to the buyer. FOB shipping point means that title passed when the goods left the seller. FOB destination means that title will pass when the goods are received by the buyer. Therefore, for inventory determination, goods in transit that are FOB shipping point should become part of the inventory, whereas those that are FOB destination should not.

Example 5.3

At the end of the year, $66,000 appears as inventory of Drew Corp. On order is another $14,000 ($10,000 FOB shipping point and $4,000 FOB destination). The inventory to be recorded is determined as:

$66,000	Inventory on hand
10,000	Ordered FOB shipping point
$76,000	Total inventory to be recorded

The $4,000 of goods ordered FOB destination will not become part of the inventory until the goods are received, as title will not pass until then to Drew Corp.

Sales

Merchandise that has already been sold but has not yet been shipped should not be considered part of the inventory figure. The same rules for goods in transit apply for sales as for purchases.

Example 5.4

A physical count of merchandise shows that $46,000 is on hand. However, $16,000 of the inventory has already been sold by Mudd but has not as yet been shipped. Since inventory is an asset, Mudd does not own and cannot record $46,000 of merchandise inventory, but only $30,000, the amount that is actually owned.

Consignment

Only inventory that is owned by the firm should be recorded. For example, merchandise on consignment would not be counted, as it is not owned by the business, but rather by the company that shipped it.

Inventory Measurement

To approach the problem of inventory measurement, in order to assign the business cost to each item, four methods of valuation (FIFO, LIFO, weighted average, and specific identification) have been developed and approved by GAAP (generally accepted accounting principles). Table 5.1 compares the first three methods with a description of specific identification discussed later in the chapter.

Table 5.1

DATE	TYPE	UNITS	UNIT COST	TOTALS
1/1	Inventory	100	$6	$ 600
3/10	Purchase	150	$8	$1,200
6/6	Purchase	200	$9	$1,800
10/4	Purchase	250	$10	$2,500
Available for sale		700		$6,100

It is to be assumed that a physical count of inventory as of the last day of the accounting period (12/31) showed 320 units on hand. Therefore, 380 units were sold during the year.

Costing Inventory: First-In-First-Out (FIFO)

This method of costing inventory makes the assumption that goods are sold in the order in which they are purchased. Therefore, the goods that were bought first are the first goods to be sold, and the goods that remain on hand (ending inventory) are assumed to be made up of the latest costs. Therefore, for income determination, earlier costs are matched with revenue and the most recent costs are used for balance sheet valuation.

This method is consistent with the actual flow of costs, since merchandisers attempt to sell their old stock first. FIFO is the most widely used inventory valuation method of those discussed.

Example 5.5

Under FIFO, those goods left at the end of the period are considered to be those received last. Therefore, the 320 units on hand on 12/31 would be costed as follows:

Most recent purchase (10/4)	250 units @ $10 =	$2,500
Next most recent purchase (6/6)	70 units @ $9 =	630
Ending inventory	320 units	$3,130

The latest cost of the inventory consists of 250 units @ $10. However, since the ending inventory consists of 320 units, we must refer to the next most recent purchase and include 70 units at $9. Therefore, you could say that the process of determining the cost of the units on hand involves working backward through the purchases until there is sufficient quantity to cover the ending inventory count. Thus, the ending inventory would be valued at $3,130 under the FIFO method of valuation.

The cost of goods sold can be determined by subtracting the value of the ending inventory from the value of the beginning inventory ($6,100 – $3,130 = $2,970).

It should be noted that as a method of assigning costs, FIFO may be used regardless of the actual physical flow of merchandise. In a period of rising prices—inflation, for example—the FIFO method will yield the largest inventory value, thus resulting in a greater net income. Conversely, the FIFO method would produce a smaller cost of goods sold because the earlier lower costs are assigned to the cost of goods sold. Because FIFO assigns the most recent charges to inventory, the value of the ending inventory is closer to its replacement cost.

Costing Inventory: Last-In-First-Out (LIFO)

The last-in-first-out (LIFO) method of inventory measurement assumes that the most recently purchased items are to be the first ones sold and that the remaining inventory will consist of the earliest items purchased. In other words, the order in which the goods are sold is the reverse order in which they are bought. Unlike FIFO, the LIFO method specifies that the cost of inventory on hand (ending inventory) is determined by working forward from the beginning inventory through purchases until sufficient units are obtained to cover the ending inventory, the exact opposite of the FIFO method.

Example 5.6

Under LIFO, the inventory at the end of the period is considered to be merchandise purchased in the first part of the period. The cost of the ending inventory for the information in Table 5.1 would be:

Earliest purchase (1/1)	100 units @ $6 =	$ 600
Next purchase (3/10)	150 units @ $8 =	$1,200
Next purchase (6/6)	70 units @ $9 =	$ 630
Ending inventory	320 units	$2,430

Thus, ending inventory would be valued at $2,430 under the LIFO method.

A disadvantage to the LIFO method is that it does not reflect the actual physical movement of goods in the business, as most businesses do not move out their most recent purchases. Yet, firms favor this method because it matches the most recent costs against the current revenue, thereby keeping earnings from being greatly distorted by any fluctuating increases or decreases in prices. However, it sometimes allows managers to do too much maneuvering to change net income. When prices are rising, certain tax advantages are gained through LIFO because it yields a lower profit because of the higher costs of goods sold.

Example 5.7

Using Table 5.1,

	FIFO	LIFO
Sales (assumed)	$20,000	$20,000
Cost of goods sold:		
Goods available for sale	6,100	6,100
Less: ending inventory	3,130	2,430
Cost of goods sold	2,970	3,670
Gross profit	$17,030	$16,330

Therefore, as Example 5.7 depicts, LIFO produces (1) a lower ending inventory, (2) a higher cost of goods sold, and (3) a lower gross profit. FIFO will produce the opposite.

The IRS will permit companies to use LIFO for tax purposes only if they use LIFO for financial reporting purposes; however, it is allowed to report an alternative inventory amount in the notes to the financial statements. Thus, if a business uses LIFO for tax purposes, it must also report inventory and income on the same valuation basis for its financial statements. This is permitted because it affords true financial analysis by allowing comparison of one business with another business in the same industry. It should be noted that a business cannot change its inventory valuation method any time it chooses, as permission must be granted by the IRS.

Costing Inventory: Weighted Average

This inventory measurement system is based on the average cost of inventory during the period and takes into considera-tion the quantity and the price of the inventory items by assigning the same amount of cost to identical items. In other words, it spreads the total dollar cost of the goods available for sale equally among all the units. The ending inventory is determined by the fol-lowing procedure:

1. The cost of the total number of units available for sale (beginning inventory plus purchases) is divided by the total number of units available for sale.
2. The number of units in the ending inventory is multiplied by the weighted average figure.

Example 5.8

Referring to the same data in Table 5.1, the cost of the 320 units on hand would be calculated as follows:

1. $6,100 / 700 units = $8.71 unit cost
2. $8.71 × 320 units on hand = $2,787* ending inventory

*Rounded off to the highest dollar.

The cost of goods sold is then calculated by subtracting the value of the ending inventory from the total value of the inventory available for sale ($6,100 − $2,787 = $3,313).

Because there were 700 units available for sale and 320 units on hand at the end of the period, the number of units sold was determined as 380 units. Therefore another method of computation to determine the cost of goods sold would be $8.71 × 380 units = $3,310.

The average cost method is best used by firms that buy large amounts of goods that are similar in nature and stored in a common place. Grain processing, gasoline, and coal are good examples of products that could logically be costed under weighted average.

There are some limitations that should be noted in this valuation procedure. Unit cost cannot be related to any physical purchase and does not represent price changes. In those industries that are greatly affected by price and style change, this method will not yield specific cost determination.

The average cost method averages price fluctuation in determining both gross profit and inventory cost, and the results will always be the same regardless of whether price trends are rising or falling.

Comparison of Inventory Methods

The three methods described above of inventory valuation are based on an assumption as to the flow of costs. The FIFO method is based on the assumption that costs flow in the order in which they were incurred; the LIFO method assumes that costs flow in the reverse of the order in which they were incurred; and the weighted average assumes that costs should be assigned to the merchandise inventory based on an average cost per unit. Note that if the costs of all purchases remain the same, the three methods of inventory valuation will yield identical results. However, as prices never remain constant, in practice each of these methods will result in a different cost for the ending inventory.

Remember

The ending figure is subtracted from the cost of goods available for sale to arrive at the cost of goods sold. Therefore, the net income or loss will vary depending upon the inventory method chosen by the company. Also the ending inventory will vary with each method.

Since ending inventory and cost of goods sold are related in the equation

Goods available for sale – ending inventory = cost of goods sold

it can be seen that if the ending inventory is overstated, then the cost of goods sold will be understated and net profit overstated. Likewise, if inventory is understated, then cost of goods sold will be overstated and net profit understated. Clearly, the method chosen for inventory computation can have a marked effect upon the profit of a company. There is no one method that is the best, but the firm must consider the following factors to help make the decision:

1. The effect on the income statement and the balance sheet

2. The effect on taxable income
3. The effect on the selling price

The following evaluations can be made concerning the three valuation methods:

FIFO

1. Yields the lowest amount of cost of goods sold (COGS)
2. Yields the highest amount of gross profit
3. Yields the highest amount of ending inventory

Note: During a period of inflation or rising prices, the use of FIFO will have these effects, but in a declining economy the results will be reversed.

LIFO

1. Yields the highest amount of COGS
2. Yields the lowest amount of gross profit
3. Yields the lowest amount of ending inventory

Weighted Average

Yields results between FIFO and LIFO for all three concepts being reviewed.

Specific Identification

The fourth method of inventory valuation is specific identification. Specific identification is a method of valuing inventory and determining costs of goods sold by using the actual costs assigned to the units on hand and to those that were sold. In other words, the actual costs of the specific items sold constitute the cost of goods sold.

Under this method, it is necessary for the business to keep records of the purchase price of each specific unit, keep records of each specific unit sold, and determine the ending inventory by totaling the cost of all the specific items on hand at the end of the period. This system is ideal for small inventories of specifically identifiable items such as houseboats or airplanes. It also gives the business the most accurate way of evaluating its inventory because actual costs, and not valuations, are used to determine the amount of the merchandise on hand at the end of the accounting period.

When the cost of administering the specific identification method becomes too high in money and time, firms usually revert to the systems discussed previously. However, even though many units are bought and sold, as long as they can be specifically identified, this method can be justified.

Example 5.9

	Units	Unit cost	Total cost
Jan 1 Beginning inventory	10	$15	$150
Mar 10 Purchase	20	18	$360
June Sales	(8)		
	22		$510

Assuming that six out of the eight sold during June were from the beginning inventory and the other two were from the March 10 purchase, the cost of goods sold would be as follows:

Jan 1	6 units	@	$15 = $90
Mar 10	2 units	@	$18 = $36
	8 units sold costing		$126

Thus the cost of goods sold would be $126, the ending inventory would be $384 ($510 − $126), and the number of units on hand would be 22 (30 − 8).

Summary

1. When inventory is recorded based upon a physical count at the end of the accounting period, it is called the _____ method.
2. The inventory method used when units are generally few in number but high in value is the _____ method.

3. The _____ method is most commonly used in retail establishments.

4. A method of inventory valuation based on the concept that goods are sold in the order in which they are received is known as _____.

5. The valuation method based on the concept that the most recent costs incurred should be charged against income is known as _____.

6. In a market of rising prices, net income under _____ will be smaller, thus producing lower tax liability.

7. The valuation method based on the concept that the unit cost of merchandise sold is the average of all expenditures for inventory is known as _____.

Answers: 1. Periodic; 2. Perpetual; 3. Periodic; 4. FIFO; 5. LIFO; 6. LIFO; 7. Weighted average

Solved Problems

5.1   (a)   Based upon the following records, determine the value of the inventory to be recorded.

Goods on hand (paid)	$59,000
Goods on hand (owed)	42,000
Goods on hand (consignment)	15,000
Goods ordered but not yet received (FOB sh.pt.)	24,000
Goods ordered but not yet received (FOB dest.)	12,000
	$152,000

(b)   How is this value treated?

SOLUTION

(a)   The inventory is valued as follows:

Goods on hand (paid)	$59,000
Goods on hand (owed)	42,000
Goods ordered (FOB sh. pt.)	24,000
Total inventory on hand	$125,000

(b)   Balance Sheet
             Current Assets
                      Merchandise Inventory $125,000

5.2 The beginning inventory and various purchases of product B were as follows:

Jan. 1	Balance	8 units @	$10.00
Mar. 5	Purchase	12 units @	11.00
June 9	Purchase	16 units @	12.00
Aug. 20	Purchase	15 units @	13.00
Nov. 1	Purchase	18 units @	14.00

An inventory count under the periodic system disclosed that 30 units of product B were on hand. Determine the ending inventory cost by (a) first-in-first-out; (b) last-in-first-out; (c) weighted average.

SOLUTION

(a)	Most recent purchase (Nov. 1)	18 units @ $14 = $252
	Next most recent (Aug. 20)	12 units @ 13 = 156
	Total Units	30 Total Cost $408
(b)	Earliest cost (Jan. 1)	8 units @ $10 = $ 80
	Next earliest (Mar. 5)	12 units @ 11 = 132
	Next earliest (June 9)	10 units @ 12 = 120
	Total Units	30 Total Cost $332
(c)		8 units @ $10 = $ 80
		12 units @ 11 = 132
		16 units @ 12 = 192
		15 units @ 13 = 195
		18 units @ 14 = $252
		69 Total Cost $851
	Total Units	30 Total Cost $370*

The weighted average cost per unit is $851 \times 69 = 12.33. The cost of 30 units on hand is calculated as $12.33 x 30 = $370*.

5.3 Determine the gross profit under the (a) FIFO and (b) LIFO assumptions, given the following information:

Sales	$40,000
Goods available for sale	12,000
Ending inventory (under FIFO)	3,500
Ending inventory (under LIFO)	6,500

SOLUTION

		FIFO		**LIFO**
Sales		$40, 000		$40, 000
Cost of Goods Sold:				
Goods Available for Sale	$12,000		$12,000	
Less End. Inventory	3,500		6,500	
Cost of Goods Sold		8,500		5,500
Gross Profit		$31,500		$34,500

Since FIFO produced a lower ending inventory, the corresponding profit was lower. Also, as a proof, FIFO produced a higher cost of goods sold, therefore yielding a lower gross profit.

Chapter 6
ALTERNATIVE VALUATION METHODS

IN THIS CHAPTER:

✔ *Net Realizable Value*
✔ *Lower of Cost or Market (LCM)*
✔ *LCM—Item by Item*
✔ *LCM—Total Replacement Cost*
✔ *Gross Profit Method*
✔ *Retail Inventory Method*
✔ *Summary of Both Methods*
✔ *Summary*
✔ *Solved Problems*

Net Realizable Value

The inventory methods mentioned earlier all reported inventory at cost. When the inventory items are damaged, become obsolete, or can be replaced at prices less than original cost, it may become necessary to

73

report the inventory at an amount that is less than cost. When it appears that inventory is obsolete or damaged, it should be reported at its net realizable value, which is the amount that the inventory can be sold for (minus selling costs).

Example 6.1

Inventory with a cost of $8,000 is determined to be obsolete and can be sold for only $3,000. This inventory should be reported at its net realizable value determined by

Cost	$8,000
Less: Estimated selling price	3,000
Loss	$5,000

The above loss of $5,000 must be recognized as soon as it is known, even before the inventory is sold. The journal entry required to recognize this loss and to reduce the inventory amount would be:

Loss on write-down of Inventory*	5,000	
Inventory		5,000

*This is an expense account.

Lower of Cost or Market (LCM)

When the value of the inventory has declined below its cost, a firm may choose the lower of cost or market method. This method involves a comparison between the cost of the inventory on hand and its current replacement cost. The lower of the two amounts is then used, which is a departure from the normal historical cost principle. Any loss in value is accomplished by an adjusting entry.

This method is used because accountants generally feel that assets should be valued conservatively, thereby not overstating their true value regardless of cost. Thus, when the price of an item is below its purchase cost, market price rather than cost must be used.

There are two methods by which a business can use the LCM method. The first is the item-by-item application, the most popular, and the other is the total replacement cost.

Note!

Lower of Cost or Market:
  Reduces ending inventory to its current value
  Results in loss reported on income statement
  May be applied on either an item-by-item basis or in the
  aggregate

LCM—Item by Item

The application of the item-by-item method is illustrated below:

Example 6.2

	Quantity	Unit Price Cost	Unit Price Market	Valuation	LCM
Item A	200	2.00	2.25	Cost	$ 400
Item B	100	1.75	1.50	Market	150
Item C	150	1.80	1.00	Market	150
					$ 700

Note that without LCM the valuation of the inventory would be $845. This number can be found be multiplying the quantity by the cost.

LCM—Total Replacement Cost

Although a physical inventory is taken once a year, there are occasions when the value of the inventory must be known during the year. When interim financial statements are requested, an inventory amount must be estimated. If no physical count is taken, the amount of inventory must be estimated. Also, in the event of fire or any other casualty, an amount must be reported as a loss. Two of the most popular methods of estimating inventory are the gross profit method and the retail method.

Example 6.3

	Quantity	Unit Price Cost	Unit Price Market	Total Cost	Total Market
Item A	200	2.00	2.25	$ 400	$ 450
Item B	100	1.75	1.50	175	150
Item C	150	1.80	1.00	270	150
				$ 1,805	$ 1,350

Inventory valuation, lower of total cost or total market, is $1,350.

Gross Profit Method

This method rearranges the Cost of Goods Sold section of the income statement. As stated before, the cost of goods sold formula is:

Beginning Inventory
+ Net Purchases
Goods Available for Sale
– Ending Inventory
Cost of Goods Sold

Note that when you subtract ending inventory from the goods available for sale, the cost of goods sold is determined. Conversely, if you subtract the estimated cost of goods sold from the goods available for sale, the value of the ending inventory will result. The estimated cost of goods sold figure is arrived at by using the past year's gross profit percentage and subtracting the resulting amount from sales.

Example 6.4

During the past five years, a company's gross profit averaged 30 percent of sales. If the sales for this interim period are $70,000, and the inventory at the beginning of the period is $30,000, you would estimate the ending inventory under the gross profit method as follows:

Beginning Inventory		$30,000
Add: Net Purchases		50,000
Goods Available for Sale		$80,000
Sales	$70,000	
Estimated Gross Profit (30%)	21,000	
Estimated Cost of Goods Sold		49,000
Estimated Ending Inventory		$31,000

Retail Inventory Method

The retail inventory method of inventory costing is used by retail businesses, particularly department stores. Department stores usually determine gross profit monthly but only take a physical inventory on an annual basis.  The retail inventory method permits a determination of inventory at any time of the year and also produces a comparison of the estimated ending inventory with the physical inventory, both at retail prices. This will help to identify any inventory shortages.

This method, similar to the gross profit method previously mentioned, is used to estimate the dollar cost of the ending inventory when a physical count cannot be done, such as in the case of fire. The procedure for determination under this method is as follows:

1. Beginning inventory and purchases must be recorded at both cost and selling prices.
2. Total goods available for sale are then computed on both bases.
3. Sales for the period are deducted from the goods available for sale at selling price.
4. Ending inventory at selling price is the result of step 3. This amount is then converted to ending inventory at cost by multiplying by the appropriate markup ratio.

Example 6.5

		Cost	Selling Price
Step 1.	Beginning Inventory	$280,000	$400,000
	+ Net Purchases for Period	110,000	180,000
Step 2.	Goods Available for Sale	$390,000	$580,000

Step 3. – Net Sales for Period   <u>340,000</u>
    Ending Inventory @ selling price $240,000
Step 4.   Cost to Selling Price Ratio ($390,000 ÷ $580,000) = 67%
    Ending Inventory @ cost ($240,000 × 67%) = $160,800

In the above example, the cost percentage is 67%, which means that the inventory and purchases are marked up to yield a gross profit margin of 33%. Certainly not all items in the goods available for sale are marked up by exactly the same percentage, but it is the average. In other words, the retail method will use a percentage that represents an average of markup cost.

Summary of Both Methods

The major difference between the gross profit method and the retail method is that the former uses the historical gross profit percentage and the latter uses the percentage markup from the current period. The gross profit method uses past experience as a basis, whereas the retail method used current experience.

    The gross profit method is usually less reliable because past situations may be different from current ones. Remember that both methods are useful because they allow the accountant to prepare interim financial statements more frequently without taking the time to physically count the inventory. However, the annual physical count is necessary, as it will disclose any loss due to theft or other shrinkage.

Remember

For **estimating** ending inventory:

> Gross profit method uses historical gross profit percentages

> Retail method uses the most recent percentage markup on cost of goods sold

Summary

1. The lower the value of ending inventory, the _____ the gross profit.
2. Determining ending inventory by LCM is done at the _____ of the period.
3. When it appears that inventory is obsolete or broken, it should be reported at its _____.
4. The most common method of inventory valuation under LCM is based on the _____ price.
5. Two methods commonly used to estimate inventory amounts are the _____ and _____ methods.

Answers: 1. Lower; 2. End; 3. Net realizable value; 4. Unit; 5. Gross profit, retail

Solved Problems

6.1 Based on the data below, determine the value of the inventory at the lower of cost or market by completing the table.

Item	Units	Unit Cost	Market Value
A	100	$1.00	$1.50
B	150	4.00	4.50
C	200	6.00	5.00
D	250	8.00	7.00

Item	Units	Basis	Lower of Cost or Market
A	100		
B	150		
C	200		
D	250		

Value of inventory _____

SOLUTION

Item	Units	Basis	Lower of Cost or Market
A	100	$1.00	$ 100
B	150	4.00	600
C	200	5.00	1,000
D	250	7.00	1,750

Value of inventory $3,450

6.2 Inventory costing $12,000 has been determined to be obsolete and can now be sold only for $8,000. (a) Record the journal entry needed to record this loss. (b) If there were costs of $600 to sell the merchandise in (a), what journal entry would be needed to record this information, and (c) what is value of the inventory after the loss is considered?

SOLUTION

(a)   Loss on write-down of inventory   4,000
            Inventor   4,000
(b)   Loss on write-down of inventory   4,600
            Inventory   4,600
(c)   The value of the inventory would be calculated as

Cost	$12,000
Loss	− 4,000
	$ 8,000
Selling costs	− 600
Ending Inventory	$ 7,400

6.3 Using the following data furnished from various sources, determine the inventory of Adam Israel that was destroyed by fire, using the gross profit method.

Beginning Inventory	$20,000
Net Purchases	40,000
Net sales	65,000
Gross Profit Average	25%

SOLUTION

Inventory (beginning)		$20,000
Add: Net purchases		40,000
Goods available for sale		$60,000
Sales	$65,000	
Estimated gross profit	16,250 (65,000 x 25%)	
Estimated cost of goods sold		48,750
Estimated ending inventory		$11,250

6.4   Estimate the cost of inventory at May 31 by the retail method.

	Cost	Retail
May 1, inventory	$18,000	$24,000
May purchases	34,000	41,000
Sales for May		37,000

SOLUTION

	Cost	Retail
May 1, inventory	$18,000	$24,000
May purchases	34,000	41,000
Goods Available for sale	$52,000	$65,000
($52,000 ÷ $65,000 = 80% ratio)		
Sales for May		37,000
May 31, inventory at retail		$28,000
May 31, inventory at estimated cost	$22,400	

Chapter 7
CASH AND
ITS CONTROL

IN THIS CHAPTER:

✔ *Classification of Cash*
✔ *Controlling Cash*
✔ *Bank Statements*
✔ *Reconciling the Bank Balance*
✔ *Petty Cash*
✔ *Summary*
✔ *Solved Problems*

In most businesses, transactions involving the receipt and disbursement of cash far outnumber any other kinds of transactions. Cash is the most liquid asset and the most subject to theft and fraud. Thus, it is essential to have a system of accounting procedures that will maintain adequate control over cash.

Classification of Cash

Roughly speaking, cash is anything that a bank will accept for deposit and will credit to the depositor's account. More precisely:

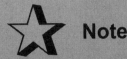

Note

A good system of cash control provides adequate procedures for protecting both cash receipts and cash disbursements. These procedures should meet these guidelines:

1. Handling of cash is separate from recordkeeping of cash
2. Cash receipts are promptly deposited in a bank.
3. Cash disbursements are made by check.

1. **Cash is a medium of exchange.** Thus, such items as currency, coin, demand deposits, savings deposits, bank drafts, personal checks, cashier's checks, and money orders are all cash. There are other items that are usually under the control of the company cashier that are not cash, such as postage stamps, post-dated checks, and IOUs. Postage is a prepaid expense, post-dated checks are receivables, and IOUs are either receivables or prepaid expenses.

2. **Cash is immediately available for payment of current debts.** Certificates of deposit (CDs) are temporary investments rather than cash, since they cannot be immediately withdrawn. Likewise, a sinking fund specifically established to pay bond requirements or a deposit with a manufacturer for purchase of equipment is not available to pay current obligations and therefore is not cash.

Controlling Cash

Cash Receipts

In a very small business the owner can maintain control through personal contact and supervision. This kind of direct intervention must, in a firm of any size, be replaced by a system of internal control, namely, the separation of duties. No person assigned to handle cash should, at the same time, be in a position to make entries in the records affecting his or her own activities.

The specific controls applied to cash receipts are as follows:

1. All receipts should be banked promptly.
2. Receipts from cash sales should be supported by sales tickets.
3. Accountability should be established each time cash is transferred.
4. Persons receiving cash should not make disbursements of cash, record cash transactions, or reconcile bank statements.

Cash Disbursements

The main ideas here are that payments should be made only by properly authorized persons, that equivalent value be received, and that documents adequately support the payment. Following are specific internal controls relating to cash disbursements:

1. All disbursements, except petty cash, should be made by prenumbered check.
2. Vouchers and supporting documents should be submitted for review when checks are signed.
3. Persons who sign checks should not have access to cash receipts, should not have custody of funds or record cash entries, and should not reconcile bank accounts.

Cash Balances

The basic principle of separation of duties is evident in the specific controls for cash balances:

1. Bank reconciliations should be prepared by persons who do not receive cash or sign checks.
2. Bank statements and paid checks should be received unopened by the person reconciling the account.
3. All cash funds on hand should be closely watched and surprise counts made at intervals.

If the requirement that all cash receipts be banked is followed, then it is clear that the monthly bank statement can be made a powerful control over cash balances.

Bank Statements

Checks

A business opens a checking account to gain the privilege of placing its deposits in a safe place and also to be able to write checks. When an account is opened, each person who is authorized to write checks on that account must sign a signature card. The bank keeps the signature card on file and compares it when checks are submitted. A check is a written notice by the depositor directing the bank to deduct a specific sum of money from the checking account and to pay that amount to the person or company written on the check. A check involves three parties:

1. **Drawer:** the one who writes the check
2. **Drawee:** the bank on which the check is drawn
3. **Payee:** the person or company to whom the check is paid

Checks offer several advantages. The checkbook stubs provide a record of the cash paid out, while the canceled checks provide proof that money has been paid to the person legally entitled to it. Also, the use of checks is the most convenient way of paying bills, because checks can safely be sent through the mail. If a check is lost or stolen, the depositors can request the bank not to pay.

Endorsements

When a check is given to the bank for deposit, the depositor signs the check to show that he or she accepts responsibility for the amount of that check. The depositor's signature is known as an endorsement. This endorsement transfers the ownership of the check and guarantees to the individual that the depositor will guarantee its payment. Different kinds of endorsements serve different needs.

1. **Blank endorsements.** This is an endorsement that consists of only the name of the endorser. Its disadvantage lies in the fact that a lost or stolen check with a blank endorsement may be cashed by the finder or thief.
2. **Endorsement in full.** This type of endorsement states that the check can be cashed or transferred only on the order of the person named in the endorsement.
3. **Restrictive endorsement.** This type of endorsement limits the receiver of the check as to the use he or she can make of the funds collected. These are usually used for checks for deposit.

Reconciling the Bank Balance

Each month, the bank forwards to the depositor a statement of his or her account showing:

1. Beginning balance
2. Deposits made and other credits
3. Checks paid and other charges (debits)
4. Ending balance

Included in this envelope with the statement are the paid or canceled checks and any other deductions or additions to the account. A deduction may be a debit memorandum for bank service charges; an addition may be a credit memorandum for the proceeds of a note collected by the bank for the depositor.

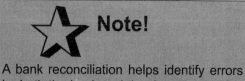

Note!

A bank reconciliation helps identify errors by both the bank and the depositor. It also identifies unrecorded items that need recording on the company's books.

Usually the balance of the bank statement and the balance of the depositor's account will not agree. To prove the accuracy of both records, the reconciling differences have to be found and any necessary entries made. The reconciling items will fall into two broad groups:

1. Those on the depositor's books but not recorded by the bank
2. Those on the bank statement but not on the depositor's books

The statement used to reconcile this difference is known as the bank reconciliation sheet.

Items on Books but Not Found on Bank Statement

Deposits in transit. These are cash receipts recorded by a company but too late to be deposited. The total of such deposits is *added* to the bank balance.

Outstanding checks. These are checks issued by the depositor but not yet presented to the bank for payment. The total of these checks is *deducted* from the bank balance.

Errors. Errors may be made in recording amounts of checks, for example a transposition of figures. The item should be added to the balance if overstated and deducted if understated.

Items on Bank Statements but Not on Books

Service charges. The bank generally deducts amounts for bank services. The exact amount is usually not known by the depositor until he or she receives the statement. The amount should be deducted from the book balance.

NSF (not sufficient funds) checks. These are checks that have been deposited but cannot be collected due to insufficient funds in the account of the drawer of the check. The bank then issues a debit memorandum charging the depositor's account. The amount should be deducted from the book balance.

Collections. The bank collects notes and other items for a small fee. The bank then adds the proceeds to the account and issues a credit memorandum to the depositor. Often there are unrecorded amounts at the end of the month. These amounts should be added to the book balance.

Errors. Journal entries should be made for any adjustments to the book accounts. Bank errors should not be entered on the books. They should be brought to the attention of the bank and corrected by the bank.

Example 7.1

The following information was available when the John Hennessey Company began to reconcile its bank balance on May 31, 19X8: balance per depositor's books, $1,638; balance per bank statement, $2,420; deposit in transit, $150; checks outstanding— #650, $300 and #654, $240; collection of $400 note plus interest of $8; collection fee for note, $10; bank service charge, $6.

John Hennessey Company
Bank Reconciliation
May 31, 19X8

Balance per bank		$2,420	Balance per checkbook		$1,638
Add: Deposit in transit		150	Add: Notes receivable	$400	
		$2,570	Interest income	8	408
					$2,046
Less:			Less:		
Outstanding checks			Collection fee	$10	
#650	$300		Service charge	6	16
#654	240	540			
Adjusted balance		$2,030	Adjusted balance		$2,030

Only reconciling items in the depositor's section (right side) are to be recorded on the books. The reconciling items in the bank section (left side) have already been recorded on the books and merely have not yet reached the bank. They will normally be included in the next bank statement.

To complete the reconcilement, the following two journal entries will be needed.

Entry 1	Cash	408	
	Notes receivable		400
	Interest income		8
Entry 2	Bank Service Expense	16	
	Cash		16

Petty Cash

Funds spent through the cash disbursements journal take the form of checks issued in payment of various liabilities. In addition, a business will have many expenditures of small amounts for which it is not practical to issue checks. Examples are postage, delivery expense, supplies, and miscellaneous small items, which are paid for in cash through a petty cash fund.

Under the so-called *imprest system*, a fund is established for a fixed petty cash amount, which is periodically reimbursed by a single check for amounts expended. The steps in setting up and maintaining the petty cash fund are as follows:

1. An estimate is made of the total of the small amounts likely to be disbursed over a short period, usually a month. A check is drawn for the estimated total and put into the fund. The only time an entry is made in the Petty Cash account is for the initial establishment of the fund, unless at some later time it is determined that this fund must be increased or decreased.

2. The individual in charge of petty cash usually keeps the money in a locked box along with petty cash vouchers. The petty cash voucher, when signed by the recipient, acts as a receipt and provides information concerning the transaction. As each payment is made, the voucher is entered in the petty cash record and placed with the balance of the money in the petty cash box.

3. Proof of petty cash is obtained by counting the currency and adding the amounts of all the vouchers in the box. The total should agree with the amount in the ledger for the petty cash fund. If it does not, the entry in the cash disbursements journal recording the reimbursement of the petty cash fund will have to include an account known as Cash Short and Over. A cash shortage is debited and a cash overage is credited to this account. Cash Short and Over is closed out at the end of the year in the Income Summary account and is treated as a general expense or miscellaneous income.

Summary

1. The most liquid asset and also the one most subject to fraud and theft is _____.
2. All disbursements, except petty cash payments, should be made by _____.
3. A check involves three parties: the _____, who writes the check; the _____, the bank on which the check is drawn; and the _____, the person or entity to whom it is to be paid.
4. The signature on the back of the check showing that the individual accepts responsibility for that amount is known as a(n) _____.
5. A bank service charge is evidenced by a(n) _____.
6. A check that has been deposited but cannot be collected by the bank because of insufficient funds is labeled _____ by the bank and is deducted from the _____ balance on a bank reconciliation.
7. Under the _____ system, a fund is established for a fixed petty cash amount, which is replenished by a single check for the total amount of amounts expended.
8. For small differences in the petty cash account, a(n) _____ account is generally used.

Answers: 1. Cash; 2. Check; 3. Drawer, drawee, payee; 4. Endorsement; 5. Debit memorandum; 6. NSF, book; 7. Imprest; 8. Cash Over and Short

Solved Problems

7.1 Based on the following information, (a) prepare a bank reconciliation and (b) journalize the adjusting entries.

1. Bank balance per statement, $7,349.46
2. Cash account balance, $5,432.76
3. Checks outstanding, $2,131.85
4. Deposit in transit not recorded by bank, $1,243.15
5. Note collected by bank, $1,015, including $15 interest
6. A check for $46 for supplies was erroneously entered as $64
7. Service charges not entered, $5

SOLUTION

(a)

Bank Reconciliation

Balance per bank statement	$7,349.46	Balance per checkbook	$5,432.76
Add: Deposit in transit	1,243.15	Add: Note collected by bank	
	$8,592.61	Note $1,000	
Less: Outstanding check	2,131.85	Interest 15	1,015.00
		Error in recording check	18.00
			$6,465.76
		Less: Service charge	5.00
Adjusted balance	$6,460.76	Adjusted balance	$6,460.76

(b)

Adjusting Entries

Cash	1,033	
Notes Receivable		1,000
Interest Income		15
Supplies		18
Bank Service Expense	5	
Cash		5

7.2 Transactions for the Eagan Company for the month of January, pertaining to the establishment of a petty cash fund, were as follows:

Jan. 1 Established an imprest petty cash fund of $50
    31 Box contained $6 cash and paid vouchers for transportation, $14; freight, $16; charity, $4; office supplies, $6; miscellaneous expense, $4

What are the journal entries necessary to record the petty cash information?

SOLUTION

Petty Cash	50	
Cash		50
Transportation Expense	14	
Freight Expense	16	
Charity Expense	4	
Office Supplies Expense	6	
Miscellaneous Expense	4	
Cash		44

Chapter 8
RECEIVABLES
AND PAYABLES

IN THIS CHAPTER:

✔ *Promissory Notes*
✔ *Computing Interest*
✔ *Accounting for Notes*
✔ *Discounting Notes*
✔ *Dishonored Notes Receivable*
✔ *Uncollectible Accounts*
✔ *Recovery of Bad Debts*
✔ *Summary*
✔ *Solved Problems*

Promissory Notes

A large portion of all business transactions are credit transactions. One way of extending credit is by the acceptance of a promissory note, a contract in which one person promises to pay another person a specific sum of money at a specific time, with or without interest. A promissory note is used for the following reasons:

1. The holder of a note can usually obtain money by taking the note to the bank and selling it (discounting the note).
2. The note is a written agreement of a debt and is better evidence than an open account.
3. It facilitates the sale of merchandise on long-term or installment plans.

For a note to be negotiable, it must meet the requirements of the Uniform Commercial Code (UCC). The requirements are:

1. The note must be in writing and signed by the maker.
2. The note must contain an order to pay a definite sum of money.
3. The note must be payable to order on demand or at a fixed future time.

You Need to Know

Interest is the charge assessed for the use of money. To a borrower, interest is an expense. To a lender, it is a revenue.

Computing Interest

For the sake of simplicity, interest is commonly computed on the basis of a 360-day year divided into 12 months of 30 days each. The basic formula is:

$$\text{Interest} = \text{Principal} \times \text{Rate} \times \text{Time}$$

Consider a note for $400 at 6 percent for 90 days. The principal is the face amount of the note ($400). The rate of interest is written as a fraction: 6 / 100. The time, if less than a year, is expressed as a fraction by placing the number of days the note runs over the number of days in a year: 90 / 360. Thus

$$\text{Interest} = \$400 \times (6/100) \times (90/360) = \$6$$

Determining Maturity Date

The maturity date is the number of specified days after the note has been issued and may be determined by:

1. Subtracting the date of the note from the number of days in the month in which it was written.
2. Adding the number of days in each of the succeeding full months, stopping with the last full month before the number of days in the note are exceeded.
3. Subtracting the total days of the result of steps 1 and 2 above from the time of the note. The resulting number is the due date in the upcoming month.

If the due date is expressed in months, the maturity date can be determined by counting that number of expressed months from the date of writing.

Accounting for Notes

Notes Payable

A promissory note is a note payable from the standpoint of the maker, whereas it is a note receivable from the standpoint of the payee. A note payable is a written promise to pay a creditor an amount of money in the future. Notes are used by a business to:

1. Make purchases
2. Settle an open account
3. Borrow money from a bank

Example 8.1

Assume that Spencer bought office equipment costing $2,000 by giving a note.

Office Equipment	2,000	
Notes Payable		2,000

There are times when a note is issued in settlement of an account payable. Assume that the Julie Agency bought merchandise from the Josh Corporation for $500 and at the end of the month, the account balance remained in full. If the Julie Agency is unable to pay, they may issue a note to the Josh Corporation for the $500 account payable, converting the account payable into a note payable. Note that the Julie Agency still owes the debt to Josh Corporation. However, it now becomes a different form of obligation, as it is a written, signed promise in the form of a note payable.

On occasion, businesses find it necessary to borrow money by giving a note payable to a bank. Frequently, banks require the interest be paid in advance. This is accomplished by deducting the amount of the interest from the principal when the loan is made and is known as *discounting a note payable*.

Notes Receivable

A note received from a customer is an asset because it becomes a claim against the buyer for the amount due.

Example 8.2

Assume that Howard Cogan owes David Smith $400 and gives him a 90-day, 12 percent note in settlement. Mr. Cogan still owes the debt, but his obligation is of a different type now. On Mr. Smith's books the entry is

Notes Receivable	400	
Accounts Receivable		400

Only the principal ($400) is recorded when the note is received, since it represents the amount of the unpaid account. The interest is not due until the date of collection, 90 days later. At that time, the interest earned will be part of the entry recognizing the receipt of the proceeds from the note:

Cash	412	
Notes Receivable		400
Interest Income*		12

*Interest = $400 \times (12/100) \times (90/360) = \$12$.

Discounting Notes

The negotiability of a note receivable enables the holder to receive cash from the bank before the due date. This is known as *discounting*. Once the interest to be paid has been determined, the procedure for discounting a note is quite simple. The *maturity value* of a note is

   1.   Face of note + interest income = maturity value.

where the face is the principal and interest income is computed as before. The holder of a note may discount it at the bank *prior to its due date*. He or she will receive the maturity value less the *discount,* or interest charge imposed by the bank for holding the note for the unexpired portion of its term. In other words

   2.   Maturity value × discount rate × unexpired time = discount.

and

   3.   Maturity value – discount = net proceeds.

Example 8.3

Mr. Ed holds a $400, 90-day, 12 percent note written by Mr. Bill on April 10. It is discounted at 12 percent on May 10. The interest on the note amounts to $12. Hence,

   1.   Maturity value = $400 + $12 = $412.

Since at the time of discounting, Mr. Ed has held the note for only 30 days, the bank will have to wait 60 days until it can receive the maturity value. The discount charge is then

2. Discount = $412 × (12/100) × (60/360) = $8.24

and Mr. Ed receives

3. Net proceeds = $412 – $8.24 = $403.76

In this example, the bank's discount rate happened to be equal to the interest rate; this need not always be the case.

Dishonored Notes Receivable

If the issuer of a note does not make payment on the due date, the note is said to be *dishonored*. It is no longer negotiable, and the amount is charged back to Accounts Receivable. The reasons for transferring the dishonored notes receivable to the Accounts Receivable accounts are that the Notes Receivable account is then limited to current notes that have not yet matured and the Accounts Receivable account will then show the dishonoring of the note, giving a better picture of the transaction.

Example 8.4

A $500, 60-day, 12 percent note written by F. Saltzman was dishonored on the date of maturity. The entry is

Accounts Receivable, F. Saltzman	510	
Notes Receivable		500
Interest Income		10

Observe that the interest income is recorded and is charged to the customer's account.

When a payee discounts a note receivable, he or she creates a contingent (potential) liability. This occurs because there is a possibility that the maker may dishonor the note. Bear in mind that the payee has already received payment from the bank in advance of the maturity date. He or she is, therefore, contingently liable to the bank to make good on the amount in the event of default by the maker. Any protest fee arising from the default of the note is charged to the maker of the note and is added to the amount to be charged against his or her account.

Uncollectible Accounts

Businesses must expect to sustain some losses from uncollectible accounts and should therefore show on the balance sheet the *net amount of accounts receivable,* the amount expected to be collected, rather than the gross amount. The difference between the gross and net amounts represents the estimated uncollectible accounts, or *bad debts.* These expenses are attributed to the year in which the sale is made, though they may be realized at a later date.

There are two methods of recording uncollectible accounts, the direct write-off method and the allowance method.

 Important Point!

The reporting of bad debts on the income statement is governed by the matching principle. This principle requires that the expenses be reported in the same period as the revenues.

Direct Write-Off Method

In small businesses, losses that arise from uncollectible accounts are recognized in the accounts *in the period in which they become uncollectible.* Under this method, when an account is deemed uncollectible, it is written off the books by a debit to the expense account, Bad Debt Expense, and a credit to the individual customer's account and to the controlling account.

Example 8.5

If Bill Anderson's $300 account receivable, dated May 15, 19X7, was deemed uncollectible in January of 19X8, the entry in 19X8 would be

Bad Debt Expense	300	
Accounts Receivable, Bill Anderson		300

It should be noted that the direct write-off method is not acceptable under GAAP, as it is not in accordance with the accrual method of accounting.

Allowance Method

As stated before, one of the fundamentals of accounting is that revenue be matched with expenses in the same year. Under the direct write-off method, in Example 8.5, the loss was not recorded until a year after the revenue had been recognized. The allowance method does not permit this. The income statement for each period  must include all losses and expenses related to the income earned in that period. Therefore, losses from uncollectible accounts should be deducted in the year in which the sale is made. Since it is impossible to predict which particular accounts will not be collected, an adjusting entry is made, usually at the end of the accounting period.

Example 8.6

Assume that in the first year of operation, a firm has estimated that $2,000 of accounts receivable will be uncollectible. The adjusting entry would be

Bad Debt Expense	2,000	
Allowance for Bad Debt		2,000

The credit balance of Allowance for Bad Debt (contra asset) appears on the balance sheet as a deduction from the total amount of Accounts Receivable:

Accounts Receivable	$30,000
Less: Allowance for Bad Debt	2,000
	$28,000

The $28,000 will become the estimated realizable value of the accounts receivable at that date. The bad debt expense will appear as an operating expense in the income statement.

Before recording the bad debt expense, a means of computing the expense should be determined. There are two generally accepted methods of calculating the amount of uncollectible accounts. One method is to use a flat percentage of the net sales for the year. The other method takes into consideration the ages of the individual accounts at the end of the fiscal year.

Percentage of Sales Method

Under the percentage of sales method, a fixed percentage of the total sales on account is taken. For example, if charge sales were $200,000 and experience has shown that approximately 1 percent of such sales will become uncollectible (or bad debts) at a future date, the adjusting entry for the bad debt account would be

Bad Debt Expense	2,000	
Allowance for Bad Debt		2,000

The same amount is used whether or not there is a balance in the Allowance for Bad Debt account. However, if any substantial balance should accumulate in the allowance account, a change in the percentage figure would become appropriate.

Balance Sheet Method

Under the balance sheet method, every account is "aged"; that is, each item in the balance is related to its sale date. The further past due the account, the more probable it is that the customer is unwilling or unable to pay. A typical analysis is shown below.

Age of Account	Accounts Receivable Balance	Estimated Percent Uncollectible	Amount
1–30 days	$ 8,000	1%	$ 80
31–60 days	12,000	3%	360
61–90 days	6,000	5%	300
91–180 days	3,000	20%	600
Over 180 days	920	50%	460
	$29,920		$1,800

The calculated allowance for uncollectible accounts ($1,800 above) is reconciled at the end of the year with the actual balance in the allowance account, and an adjusting entry is made. The amount of the adjusting entry must take into consideration the balance of the Allowance for Bad Debt account. The percentage of sales method does not follow this procedure.

Example 8.7

The analysis showed that $1,800 would be required in the Allowance for Bad Debt account at the end of the period. The Allowance for Bad Debt account had a credit balance of $200. The adjusting entry at the end of the period would be

Bad Debt Expense	1,600*	
Allowance for Bad Debt		1,600

*($1,800 – $200).

If, however, there had been a debit balance of $200, a credit to Allowance for Bad Debt account of $2,000 would be necessary to bring the closing balance to $1,800.

When it becomes evident that a customer's account is uncollectible, it is written off the books. This is done by crediting Accounts Receivable for the amount deemed uncollectible and debiting the Allowance for Bad Debt account. Note that there is no expense at this time, as it was already estimated in the previous year.

Example 8.8

John Andrews's account (a) was deemed uncollectible.

Allowance for Bad Debt	600	
Accounts Receivable, J. Andrew		600

General Ledger	Accounts Receivable Ledger

Allowance for Uncollectible Accounts		John Andrew	
(a) 600	Bal. 1,800	Bal. 600	(a) 600

Accounts Receivable	
Bal. 29,200	(a) 600

Recovery of Bad Debts

If a written-off account is later collected in full or part, *a recovery of bad debts,* the write-off will be reversed for the amount received.

Example 8.9

At a later date, Mr. Andrew (see Example 8.8) pays his account in full. The reversing entry (b) to restore his account will be

Accounts Receivable, John Andrew	600	
Allowance for Bad Debt		600

A separate entry, (c), will then be made in the cash receipts journal to record the collection, debiting Cash $600 and crediting Accounts Receivable, John Andrew. If a partial collection was made, the reversing entry should be made for the amount recovered.

General Ledger	Accounts Receivable Ledger

Cash		John Andrew	
(c) 600		Bal. 600	(a) 600
		(b) 600	(c) 600

Accounts Receivable	
29,200	(a) 600
(b) 600	(c) 600

Allowance for Uncollectible Accounts	
(a) 600	Bal. 1,800
	(b) 600

Summary

1. The practice of transferring a customer's note to a bank is called _____.

2. The face of a note plus the interest due is known as _____.

3. Under the _____ method, uncollectible accounts are charged to expense when they become uncollectible.

4. Bad Debts Expense appears in the _____, whereas Allowance for Uncollectible Accounts appears in the _____.

5. The method of estimating bad debts that is based on the age of the receivables is known as the _____ approach.

6. Ascertaining the amount and time outstanding for each account receivable is called _____.

7. If Kevin issues to Dan a $1000 note, Kevin is called the _____, and Dan is called the _____.

8. The interest on a $800, 90-day, six percent note would be _____.

9. Normally, banks will base their discount on the _____ of the note.

10. What effect does the acceptance of a note receivable generally have on the total assets of the firm? _____.

Answers: 1. Discounting; 2. Maturity value; 3. Direct write-off; 4. Income statement, balance sheet; 5. Balance sheet; 6. Aging; 7. Maker, payee; 8. $12; 9. Maturity value; 10. No effect

Solved Problems

8.1 From the following information, prepare the necessary journal entries.

1. On June 10, received a 30-day, 12 percent, $5,000 note dated June 9 from Price Rite in settlement of his account.

2. July 9, received payment from Price Rite on note.

SOLUTION

June 10	Notes Receivable	5,000	
	Accounts Receivable, Price Rite		5,000
July 9	Cash	5,050	
	Notes Receivable		5,000
	Interest Income		50

8.2 Record the following transactions in the books of Mary Sudolle Company.

(a) May 1 — Received a $6,000, 90-day, 12 percent note in settlement of the Happy Valley account

(b) May 31 — Discounted the note at 10 percent at the bank

(c) July 30 — Happy Valley paid the note in full

SOLUTION

(a)	Notes Receivable	6,000	
	Accounts Receivable, Happy Valley		6,000
(b)	Cash	6,077	
	Interest Income		77
	Notes Receivable		6,000
(c)	No entry		

8.3 Using the aging schedule below, prepare the adjusting entry providing for the uncollectible accounts expense.

Account	Age	Estimated % Uncollectible
$24,000	1-30 days	1%
18,000	31-60 days	3%
10,000	61-180 days	25%
6,000	181 days and over	60%

SOLUTION

Bad Debts Expense	6,880*	
Allowance for Bad Debt Accounts		6,880

*$ 240   1-30 days ($24,000 × 1%)
$ 540   31-60 days ($18,000 × 3%)
$2,500   61-180 days ($10,000 × 25%)
$3,600   181 days and over ($6,000 × 60%)

Chapter 9
PROPERTY, PLANT, AND EQUIPMENT: DEPRECIATION

IN THIS CHAPTER:

✔ *Fixed Assets*
✔ *Depreciation and Scrap Value*
✔ *Methods of Depreciation*
✔ *Comparison of Methods*
✔ *Summary*
✔ *Solved Problems*

Fixed Assets

Tangible assets that are relatively permanent and are needed for the production or sale of goods or services are termed *property, plant, and equipment (PP&E),* or *fixed assets.* These assets are not held for sale in the ordinary course of business and will serve the firm for more than one year. The broad group is usually separated into classes according to the physical characteristics of the items, for example, land, buildings, and machinery and equipment.

The cost of PP&E includes all expenditures necessary to put the asset into position and make it ready for use.

Example 9.1

For a lathe purchased by AB Company, the data were invoice price, $11,000; cash discount, $220; trucking, $200; installation, $720. The total cost is $11,000 − $220 + $200 + $720 = $11,700. The entry is

Machinery and Equipment	11,700	
Cash		11,700

Depreciation and Scrap Value

Though it may be long, the useful life of a fixed asset is limited. Eventually the asset will lose all productive worth and will possess only salvage value or scrap value. The accrual basis of accounting demands a period-by-period matching of costs against derived revenues. Hence the cost of a fixed asset (over its scrap value) is distributed over the asset's entire estimated lifetime. This spreading of the cost over the periods that receive benefits is known as *depreciation*.

To determine depreciation expense for a fixed asset, we need the following information:

1. **Cost.** The total purchase price of the item, as described above.
2. **Estimated Useful Life.** The projected life during which the business expects the asset to function. This may be expressed in years, miles, units of production, or any other appropriate measure.
3. **Residual Value.** Also called scrap value, the estimated value of the asset when it is fully depreciated. When subtracted from the cost of the asset, it produces the "depreciable cost."

Depreciation decreases the fixed asset's book value and also decreases owner's equity. Depreciation is considered an operating expense of the business. It may be recorded by an entry at the end of each month or at the end of the year, usually depending on the frequency of preparing financial statements. Fixed assets are recorded at cost and remain at that figure as long as they are held. The depreciation taken to date is shown as a credit in the contra asset account Accumulated Depreciation and is deducted from the asset account on the balance sheet.

Example 9.2

Equipment	$10,000
Less: Accumulated Depreciation	4,000
	$6,000

The book value of the equipment has gone from $10,000 to $6,000.

There is one exception to the above considerations: land. This fixed asset is non-depreciable and is carried on the books at full cost.

Methods of Depreciation

The depreciable amount of a fixed asset—that is, cost minus scrap value—may be written off in different ways. The amount may be spread evenly over the years, as in the straight-line method, or it may be accelerated. Two accelerated methods are the double-declining balance and the sum-of-the-years'-digits method. These methods provide for larger amounts of depreciation in the earlier years. Repairs, on the other hand, are generally lower in earlier years, so the total cost of depreciation and repairs should be about the same each year. The units-of-production method bases depreciation each period on the amount of output.

Straight-Line

The straight-line method is the simplest and most widely used depreciation method. Under this method, an equal portion of the cost of the asset is allocated to each period of use. The periodic charge is expressed as

$$\frac{\text{Cost} - \text{scrap value}}{\text{Useful life (in years)}} = \text{Annual Depreciation Charge}$$

Example 9.3

Cost of machine, $17,000; scrap value, $2,000; estimated useful life, 5 years.

$$\frac{\$17,000 - \$2,000}{5 \text{ years}} = \$3,000 \text{ per year}$$

The entry to record the depreciation would be

Depreciation Expense, Machinery	3,000	
Accumulated Depreciation, Machinery		3,000

Book value should not be confused with market value. The book value is the difference between cost and accumulated depreciation. Market value is what the asset can actually be sold for on a given date. As an asset is used, accumulated depreciation increases and book value decreases.

You Need to Know

In the final year of the asset's useful life, book value is the same as the scrap value. At this point, the asset is said to be fully depreciated.

If an asset is held for more than half a month, that month is counted. If it is held for less than 15 days in a month, that month is not counted. An asset bought on or before the 15th of the month is considered to be in use and therefore can be depreciated for the entire month. If it is bought on or after the 16th, it cannot be depreciated for that month and depreciation will begin in the next month.

Example 9.4

A truck bought on April 6, is depreciated for 9 months, April through December. But if the truck is bought on April 16, depreciation is calculated for only 8 months, May through December. After this first partial year, the truck is depreciated for each remaining full 12-month year until it is fully depreciated.

Units-of-Production (UOP)

Units-of-production depreciation is based on an asset's usage. This can be expressed in

1. Units produced
2. Hours consumed
3. Mileage driven

This method is used when an asset's usage varies from year to year. Under the first variation of the UOP method, a fixed amount of depreciation is allocated to each unit of output produced by the machine. The per-unit depreciation expense is multiplied by the number of units produced in each accounting period. This depreciation method accurately reflects the depreciation expense for the asset because it is based on the number of units produced in each period. Depreciation per unit is computed in two steps:

1.
$$\frac{\text{Cost of asset} - \text{scrap value}}{\text{Total estimated units of output}} = \text{Depreciation per unit}$$

2. Units produced × unit depreciation = annual depreciation expense

Example 9.5

Cost of machine, $17,000; scrap value, $2,000; total estimated units produced during lifetime, 300,000.

First-year production	25,000 units
Second-year production	30,000 units

The depreciation expense for the first and second years would be calculated as follows:

$$\frac{\$17{,}000 - \$2{,}000}{300{,}000} = \$.05 \text{ depreciation per unit}$$

Year 1: 25,000 units × $.05 = $1,250
Year 2: 30,000 units × $.05 = $1,500

In the second variation of UOP, a fixed amount of depreciation is allocated, based on the number of hours the machine is used.

Example 9.6

Determine the depreciation for the following machines in the first year using the straight-line method and the UOP hours-of-usage method:

	Machine A	Machine B
Cost	$22,000	$22,000
Scrap Value	$ 2,000	$ 2,000
Estimated Life	5 years	5 years
	(18,000 hours)	(18,000 hours)

Machine A was in use for 3,000 hours in the first year
Machine B was in use for 1,000 hours in the first year

Straight-line Depreciation = $4,000 annual depreciation expense*
*($22,000 – $2,000) / 5 years = $4,000

UOP hours of usage = $1.11 annual depreciation expense*
*($22,000 – $2,000) / 18,000 hours = $1.11

Machine A = 3,000 hours × $1.11 = $3,330 first-year depreciation expense
Machine B = 1,000 hours × $1.11 = $1,110 first-year depreciation expense

The difference between the first-year depreciation using the straight-line method and that using the UOP method is considerable. Under the UOP method, machine B's limited use results in its having one third the depreciation expense of machine A. Under the straight-line method, both machines carry the same depreciation expense, regardless of use. In this case, UOP is the more logical choice for reporting depreciation because it more accurately matches expense against periodic income.

Under the third variation of UOP depreciation, instead of using time to calculate depreciation, the number of miles driven are the "units." The depreciation expense per mile will remain constant over the life of the truck, and will be multiplied by the actual miles the truck is driven in each accounting period.

Example 9.7

A truck costing $24,000 with salvage value of $4,000 has an estimated useful life of 80,000 miles. If, in the first year, it is driven 18,000 miles, what is the entry needed to record depreciation expense?

$$\frac{\$24,000 \text{ (cost)} - \$4,000 \text{ (salvage value)}}{80,000 \text{ total estimated miles}} = \$.25 \text{ per mile}$$

18,000 (miles driven) @ $.25 = $4,500 first-year depreciation expense

Depreciation Expense, Truck	4,500	
Accumulated Depreciation, Truck		4,500

Double-Declining Balance

Double-declining balance is an accelerated method of depreciation because a greater amount of depreciation expense is taken in the early years of an asset's life and less is taken in later years. This method is preferred for the following reasons:

1. Technology can make an asset obsolete or inadequate before the asset wears out.
2. Most plant assets decline in value more quickly in their early years than in later years.
3. Often, an asset contributes most to a business during its first years.
4. The expenditure for equipment is made at the beginning of the asset's life.

5. It is good accounting practice to charge more depreciation in the early years of an asset's useful life.

The double-declining balance (DDB) method produces the highest amount of depreciation in earlier years. It does not recognize scrap value. Instead, the book value of the asset remaining at the end of the depreciation period becomes the scrap value. Under this method, the straight-line rate is doubled and applied to the declining book balance each year. Many companies prefer the double-declining balance method because of the faster write-off in the earlier years when the asset contributes the most to the business and when the expenditure was actually made. The procedure is to apply a fixed rate to the declining book value of the asset each year. As the book value declines, the depreciation becomes smaller.

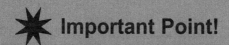 **Important Point!**

Depreciation is a process of cost allocation rather than valuation. Plant assets are reported on balance sheets at their remaining undepreciated costs (book value), not at market values.

Example 9.8

A $17,000 asset is to be depreciated over 5 years. The double-declining balance rate is thus 40 percent per year.

Year	Book Value at Beginning of Year	Rate	Depreciation for Year	Book Value at End of Year
1	$17,000	40%	$6,800	$10,200
2	10,200	40%	4,080	6,120
3	6,120	40%	2,448	3,672
4	3,672	40%	1,469	2,203
5	2,203	40%	881	1,322

The $1,322 book value at the end of the fifth year becomes the scrap value. If however, a scrap value of $2,000 had been estimated, the depreciation for the fifth year would be $203 ($2,203 – $2,000) instead of $881. The date of purchase should also be considered. Up to this point it has been assumed that the equipment was purchased at the beginning of the year, which is usually not the case. Therefore a change in the computation for the first partial year is needed.

Example 9.9

If in Example 9.8 the equipment had been purchased and placed into use at the end of the sixth month of the fiscal year, the pro rata portion of the first full year's depreciation would be

$$1/2 \times (40\% \times \$17,000) = \$1,700$$

The method of computation for the remaining years would not be affected. Thus

$$40\% \times (\$17,000 - \$1,700) = \$6,120$$

would be the depreciation for the second year and $9,180 its book value.

Sum-of-the-Years'-Digits

The fourth method of computing depreciation is sum-of-the-years'-digits. Like DDB, it is an accelerated method that allows more depreciation expense to be recorded in the early years of an asset's life and less in the later years. As with DDB, depreciation expense declines over the life of the asset; however, unlike the case with DDB, it declines by the same amount each year. This method's use is extremely rare.

Comparison of Methods

Once you know the four methods of depreciation, the next question is how to select the one that's most appropriate. Under generally accepted accounting principles (GAAP), businesses are encouraged to match the income an asset produces against its expense. This can be accomplished by selecting the correct depreciation method.

Of the four depreciation methods discussed earlier, three are compared in the table below. It is assumed that over a 5-year lifetime the asset was in operation for the following numbers of hours: 1,800, 1,200, 2,000, 1,400, and 1,600. Cost of asset, $17,000; scrap value, $2,000.

Table 9.1

YEAR	SL	UOP	DDB
1	$ 3,000	$ 3,375	$ 6,800
2	3,000	2,250	4,080
3	3,000	3,750	2,448
4	3,000	2,625	1,468
5	3,000	3,000	204
Total	$ 15,000	$ 15,000	$ 15,000

Based upon Table 9.1 we can conclude the following:

1. If the asset is expected to generate income evenly over an extended period of time, the *straight-line method* should be used.
2. If the asset will produce a different number of units each year, or if the machine may wear out early, the *units-of-production method* is preferable because it is based upon the usage rather than time.
3. If the asset is expected to generate high income in its early years, the *double-declining balance method* should be used because it will generate greater depreciation expense in its earlier years, as it can be matched with the early period's higher revenues, or because it is closer to the date of purchase when the major expenditure was made. This accelerated depreciation method reduces tax liability in the early years, making more cash available for the asset's purchase.

Summary

1. Accumulated Depreciation is an example of a(n) _____ account, since the fixed asset remains at cost while this account builds up.

2. The market value of a fixed asset at the end of its useful life is known as _____.
3. The uniform distribution of depreciation over the life of an asset is known as the _____ method.
4. The method that produces the largest amount of depreciation in the earlier years, then rapidly declines, is known as the _____ method.
5. When income produced by an asset each year is the same, the recommended method of depreciation is _____.
6. Where use, rather than time, is the key factor, _____ is the preferred method of depreciation.

Answers: 1. Contra or offset; 2. Salvage value or residual value; 3. Straight-line; 4. Double-declining-balance; 5. Straight-line; 6. Units-of-production

Solved Problems

9.1 Hacol Company acquired an asset on January 1, 19X8, at a cost of $38,000, with an estimated useful life of 8 years and a salvage value of $2,000. What is the annual depreciation based on the straight-line method?

SOLUTION

Cost	$38,000	
Scrap Value		2,000
Amount to be depreciated		$36,000

9.2 For the asset of Problem 9.1, compute the depreciation for the first two years by using the double-declining balance method.

SOLUTION

For the depreciation rate, we take twice the straight-line rate; that is,

$$2 \times (100\% / 8 \text{ years}) = 25\% \text{ per year}$$

Therefore,

Year 1: $38,000 \times 25\% = \$9,500$
Year 2: $(\$38,000 - \$9,500) \times 25\% = \$7,125$

9.3 A machine was purchased for $28,000 and had an estimated scrap value of $4,000 and an estimated life of 32,000 hours. What would the year-end entry be if the units-of-production method was used, and it was used 7,200 hours in the first year of operation?

SOLUTION

Depreciation Expense, Machine	5,400*	
Accumulated Depreciation, Machine		5,400

*($28,000 – 4,000) / 32,000 hours est. life = 0.75 × 7200 hours = $5400

Chapter 10
PROPERTY, PLANT, AND EQUIPMENT: DISPOSAL AND TAXATION

IN THIS CHAPTER:

✔ *Disposals of Fixed Assets*
✔ *Depreciation and Income Taxes*
✔ *Summary*
✔ *Solved Problems*

Disposals of Fixed Assets

Plant assets get old, eventually wear out, and must be replaced. When this occurs, the business disposes of the asset. Regardless of the method used, the asset and its related accumulated depreciation must be removed from the accounts upon disposal. The accumulated depreciation account is debited and the asset is credited for its cost.

Accounting procedures for the disposal of a plant asset vary depending on how the asset is disposed of. Three methods will be described here:

1. Retiring (discarding) the asset
2. Selling the asset
3. Exchanging the asset

When plant assets are no longer needed, they may be sold for scrap or they may simply be discarded. Sometimes, an asset is fully depreciated but remains in operation. Even though it has completed its estimated useful life for accounting purposes, it may still remain functional for the business. When this occurs, the asset and related accumulated depreciation accounts remain in the ledger to reflect the asset's continued use. Because the disposal date usually does not coincide with the date when depreciation is recorded, depreciation expense must be brought up to date before writing off the asset.

You Need to Know

Before retiring, selling, or trading in the asset, entries must be made for unrecorded depreciation that has accrued since the last depreciation expense was entered.

Example 10.1

A $15,000 asset with accumulated depreciation of $12,600 had been depreciated at the annual rate of 10 percent. If we decide to discard the asset on April 30, an adjusting entry is needed to record the depreciation for the period from January 1 to April 30, since no entry to record the expense has been made. Therefore, one third of the annual depreciation of $1,500 ($15,000 × 10%) must be recorded.

Entry 1	Depreciation Expense	500	
	Accumulated Depreciation		500

The entry is necessary to bring the accumulated depreciation up to the date of disposal. The entry to record this disposal of the asset would be

Entry 2	Accumulated Depreciation	13,100	
	Loss on Disposal of Asset	1,900	
	Equipment		15,000

Retiring an asset literally means junking it. But a sale, no matter how small, usually involves a cash transaction. If the selling price is greater than the book value, a gain on sale results. If the selling price is less than the book value, there is a loss. If the asset is sold for book value there is no gain or loss.

The entry to record the sale of an asset is similar to the one for disposal except that an entry must be made to show that compensation has been received. The sale requires entries to bring the depreciation up to date, and to record the sale at either a gain or a loss.

Example 10.2

A $15,000 asset with accumulated depreciation of $12,600 as of December 31, and an estimated straight-line life of 10 years, is sold on the following April 30 for $2,300.

Entry 1	Depreciation Expense	500*	
	Accumulated Depreciation		500
*1/3 × $1,500			

Entry 2	Cash	2,300	
	Accumulated Depreciation	13,100	
	Equipment		15,000
	Gain on Disposal of Asset		400

Example 10.3

Assume the same information as in Example 10.2 except that the equipment was sold for $1,600.

Entry 1	Depreciation Expense	500	
	Accumulated Depreciation		500

Entry 2	Cash	1,600	
	Accumulated Depreciation	13,100	
	Loss on disposal of asset	300	
	Equipment		15,000

Instead of either retiring or selling old plant assets, businesses often exchange them for similar assets that are more efficient. This exchange, known as a trade-in, is subtracted from the new asset's price, and the balance that remains (known as "boot") will be paid based on the terms of the agreement. To record this trade-in, the firm must remove the asset's balance and its related accumulated depreciation account from the books. The trade-in allowance can be greater or less than the book value of the old asset being exchanged. In past years, it was an acceptable practice to recognize the difference between book value and trade-in as a gain or loss, but today only losses maybe recognized.

Nonrecognition of Gain. The way to record a gain from an exchange of similar assets is to absorb it into the cost of the new asset. This requires several steps:

Step 1. Determine the book value of the old asset by subtracting the accumulated depreciation from its cost.
Step 2. Determine the boot by subtracting the old asset's trade-in allowance from the new asset's list price.
Step 3. Calculate the depreciable cost of the new asset by adding the book value of the old asset to the boot.

Example 10.4

Data:

Old Equipment			New Equipment	
Step 1:			Step 2:	
Cost	$15,000	Price		$20,000
Accum. Depr.	12,600	Trade-in		2,500
Depr. for current		Cash to be paid		$17,500
Year	500	$13,100		
Book value		$ 1,900		

Step 3:

Book value	$ 1,900
Boot	<u>17,500</u>
New equipment	$19,400

Entry 1 Depreciation expense	500	
Accumulated Depreciation		500

Entry 2 Accumulated Depreciation	13,100	
Equipment (new)	19,400	
Equipment (old)		15,000
Cash		17,500

Even though this transaction yields a gain of $600, GAAP does not permit the business to recognize it. This is based on the idea that income is generated by the sale of items that an asset produces, not from the sale of the asset itself. The gain of $600 that is not recognized will be matched by a reduction of $600 in the total depreciation expense over the life of the equipment, resulting in lower depreciation expense in future years.

Recognition of Loss. If less is received for an old asset than is paid for the new one, the loss may be recognized for accounting purposes, but not for tax purposes. In other words, there is one set of rules for financial statements and another set of rules for tax returns.

Example 10.5

Using the information from the previous example, assume that the trade-in allowance was $1,000 instead of $2,500. The entries that are required would be

Entry 1 Depreciation expense	500	
Accumulated Depreciation		500

Entry 2 Accumulated Depreciation	13,100	
Equipment (new)	20,000	
Loss on disposal of asset	900	

Equipment (old)	15,000
Cash	19,000

Nonrecognition of Loss. Since federal income tax law permits neither gains nor losses on exchanges of similar assets, no loss account may be used for tax purposes, even thought it was used for accounting. The new cost will be determined by adding the boot to the book value of the old equipment. In the previous example, the new equipment would have been recorded with a book value of $20,900.

Assets Dissimilar in Nature. For trade-ins of assets that are dissimilar, such as the exchange of a truck for a printing press, both gains and losses are recognized.

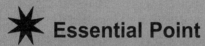

Essential Point

The gain or loss can be determined by comparing the book value of the assets given up with the fair market value of the assets received.

Example 10.6

A truck that cost $14,000 and has updated accumulated depreciation of $10,000 is exchanged for a printing press costing $15,000. The truck receives a trade-in allowance of $6,000, with the balance to be paid in cash. What entry is required to record this?

Step 1:	Cost of the truck	$ 14,000
	Less: Accum. Depr.	10,000
	Book value of truck	$ 4,000
Step 2:	Cost of printing press	$ 15,000
	Less: Trade-in allowance	6,000
	Cash to be paid (boot)	$ 9,000

Step 3:	Book value of the truck	$ 4,000	
	Less: Trade-in allowance	6,000	
	Gain on trade-in	$ 5,000	

Entry:

	Printing Press	15,000	
	Accumulated Depreciation	10,000	
	Truck		14,000
	Cash		9,000
	Gain on Trade-in		3,000

Depreciation and Income Taxes

Accelerated Cost Recovery System (ACRS)

Although the accelerated methods of depreciation—double-declining balance and the sum-of-the-years'-digits—produce more depreciation expense than straight-line in the early years of an asset's life, many firms wanted even faster write-offs. To meet this demand, Congress included the ACRS system in the 1981 tax reform. It permitted even faster depreciation write-offs for federal income tax purposes, but only for assets  placed in use after 1980. Assets purchased before 1981 were limited to one of the other accelerated depreciation methods. ACRS is easier to compute than double-declining balance because it does not recognize scrap value or trade-in or allow partial depreciation for assets bought during the year. Assets purchased under ACRS from 1981 to 1986 were classified according to an estimated recovery period:

Three years: autos, light trucks, and machinery used for research
Five years: heavy trucks, ships, aircraft, office furniture and equipment, and anything that does not fall into another category
Ten years: railroad tank cars, residential mobile homes, and certain public utility property
Fifteen years: other public utility property
Fifteen – Nineteen years: residential and commercial property

Example 10.7

A car was purchased in 1984 for $25,000. The depreciation expense allowed each year under ACRS would be computed as follows. According to the list above, autos fall into the three-year class of ACRS. Therefore, the following depreciation expense would be recorded for each year:

1984:	25% × $25,000 =	$ 6,250
1985:	38% × $25,000 =	$ 9,500
1986:	37% × $25,000 =	$ 9,250
Total depreciation		$25,000

Note:
1. At the end of 1986, the cost of the auto has been fully recovered.
2. No scrap value was used.
3. Because ACRS allocated depreciation over a much shorter period of time than the asset's true life, it was acceptable only for tax purposes, not for preparing financial statements.

Modified Accelerated Cost Recovery System (MACRS)

Five years after creating ACRS, Congress modified it in the famous Tax Reform Act of 1986. This law permits a modified ACRS for assets purchased after December 31,1986. It kept four classes of depreciable assets and added four more classes: 7 years, 20 years, 27.5 years, and 31.5 years. It also changed the recovery periods for a number of assets. Cars and light trucks were changed from three years to five years, and office equipment and furniture went from five years to seven years.

In the MACRS table below, there appears to be an extra year in each class. This extra period is based on "the half-year convention," which assumes that all assets are actually placed in service in the middle of the year and taken out of service in the middle of the year. Thus, neither the first nor the last year of depreciation in any class is considered a full year. An extra year is added to each asset's depreciation expense: a three-year asset is depreciated over four years.

Modified Accelerated Cost Recovery System

Recovery year	Recovery periods					
	3 years	5 years	7 years	10 years	15 years	20 years
1	33.3%	20.00%	14.29%	10.00%	5.00%	3.750%
2	44.45	32.00	24.49	18.00	9.50	7.219
3	14.81	19.20	17.49	14.40	8.55	6.677
4	7.41	11.52	12.49	11.52	7.70	6.177
5		11.52	8.93	9.22	6.93	5.713
6		5.76	8.92	7.37	6.23	5.285
7			8.93	6.55	5.90	4.888
8			4.46	6.55	5.90	4.522
9				6.56	5.91	4.462
10				6.55	5.90	4.461
11				3.28	5.91	4.462
12					5.90	4.461
13					5.91	4.462
14					5.90	4.461
15					5.91	4.462
16					2.95	4.461
17						4.462
18						4.461
19						4.462
20						4.461
21						2.231

Note: The 27.5-year class for residential rental property and 31.5-year class for nonresidential real property are not included here for reasons of space. Special rules apply to real estate.

Summary

1. Depreciation is considered a(n) _____ expense because it does not drain cash from operations.
2. The rapid write-off system introduced in the Economic Recovery Tax Act in 1981 is known as _____.
3. The rapid write-off system that replaced that in question 2 is known by what initials? _____
4. Under this system, all assets are assumed to be placed in service in the _____ of the year of acquisition.

5. The common business term for the exchange of similar assets is _____.

6. The balance to be paid after deducting the trade-in allowance from the price of a new asset is called the _____.

7. GAAP do not permit recognition of a gain on the exchange of _____ assets.

8. If a trade-in of similar assets results in a loss, the loss may be recognized for _____ purposes but not for _____ purposes.

Answers: 1. Noncash; 2. Accelerated Cost Recovery System (ACRS); 3. MACRS; 4. mid-point; 5. Trade-in; 6. Boot; 7. Similar; 8. Book, tax

Solved Problems

10.1 As of December 31, 19X8, accumulated depreciation of $9,000 has been recorded on equipment that originally cost $14,000. What is the entry to record the disposal of the asset if the equipment was discarded with no salvage value?

SOLUTION

Accumulated Depreciation, Equipment	9,000	
Loss on Disposal of Fixed Assets	5,000	
Equipment		14,000

10.2 For problem 10.1, what entry would be recorded if the equipment was sold for $6,000?

SOLUTION

Accumulated Depreciation, Equipment	9,000	
Cash	6,000	
Equipment		14,000
Gain on Disposal of Fixed Assets		1,000*

*Cost	$14,000	Cash Sale	$6,000
Accumulated Depreciation	9,000	Book value	5,000
Book value	$ 5,000	Gain	$1,000

10.3 Kevin Staton Company traded in a cutting machine for a new one priced at $2,600, receiving a trade-in allowance of $600 and paying the balance in cash. The old machine cost $1,800 and had an accumulated depreciation of $1,400. What is the entry to record the acquisition of the new machine?

SOLUTION

Accumulated Depreciation, Machine	1,400	
Machine (new)	2,400*	
Machine (old)		1,800
Cash		2,000

*Price of new machine	$2,600
Less: Unrecognized gain	200
Cost of new machine	$2,400

Chapter 11
CAPITAL AND EQUITY

IN THIS CHAPTER:

✔ Sole Proprietorships
✔ Partnerships
✔ Corporations
✔ Summary
✔ Solved Problems

Sole Proprietorships

A sole proprietorship is a business owned by one individual. It is a separate business entity, but it is not a separate legal entity. The proprietor owns the assets and owes the creditors personally, not as a business, as in the case of a corporation.

The equity of the sole proprietor consists of three accounts: an owner's equity account, a drawing account, and an income summary account. These accounts are described and illustrated below.

Owner's equity account. The owner's equity account (also known as the proprietor's capital account) reflects the changes in his or her equity during the year.

Example 11.1

On January 1, Casey Mudd invested $10,000 in his business.

Jan. 1   Cash   10,000
           Casey Mudd, Capital   10,000

Drawing Account. Before earnings are made, the proprietor usually has to draw compensation for his living expenses. He is not an employee, and therefore does not earn a salary; his earnings result from profits of the company. Such drawings reduce his equity and reduce cash.

Example 11.2

Casey Mudd decides that he will withdraw $500 a month for personal expenses. He expects this equity reduction to be more than offset by his earnings, which will be determined at the end of the year.

Casey Mudd, Drawing   500
     Cash   500

The account Casey Mudd, Drawing is used to accumulate the details of the drawings so that only one figure, the total, is transferred to the capital account at the end of the year. When the drawings of $6,000 for the year are transferred, the entry is as follows:

Dec. 31 Casey Mudd, Capital   6,000
           Casey Mudd, Drawing   6,000

Income summary account. When the accounts are summarized and closed, the various expenses are debited in total to Income Summary and the individual expense accounts are credited. The revenue is credited in total to Income Summary and the individual revenue accounts are debited. The net difference, a profit or a loss, is transferred to the capital account.

Example 11.3

The business of Casey Mudd had revenues from fees of $20,000 and expenses of $9,000. The revenue of $20,000, less total expenses of $9,000, results in net income of $11,000. The account is closed out and the balance transferred to the capital account with the following entry:

Dec. 31 Income Summary   11,000
            Casey Mudd, Capital   11,000

The account Casey Mudd, Capital will now reflect the proprietor's investment, drawings, and income:

<u>Casey Mudd, Capital</u>

Dec 31, 19X8 Drawing	6,000 | Jan 1, 19X8 Investment	10,000
31, 19X8 Balance	<u>15,000</u> | Net income	<u>11,000</u>
	$ 21,000 |	$ 21,000
	| Jan 1, 19X9 Balance	$ 15,000

Instead of showing a single capital item on the closing balance sheet, it is preferable to present the opening balance, the increase and decrease for the period, and the closing balance, as shown below.

Owner's Equity

Casey Mudd, Capital		
Balance January 1, 19X8		$10,000
Net income for year	$11,000	
Drawings for year	<u>6,000</u>	<u>5,000</u>
Balance, December 31, 19X8		$15,000

 **Note**

If a business is a sole proprietorship, the equity section consists of a single line showing the owner's equity as of the balance sheet date.

Partnerships

A partnership, according to the Uniform Partnership Act, is "an association of two or more persons to carry on as co-owners of a business for profit." Such an association should preferably be expressed in a partnership agreement. Profits may be shared equally, according to invested capital, or on any other basis. A partner's share is called his or her interest in the business.

The partnership capital accounts consist of a capital account for each partner, a drawing account for each partner, and an income summary account. The capital accounts and the drawing accounts serve the same role as the capital and drawing accounts in a sole proprietorship and are treated in a like manner. The income summary account is treated slightly differently.

Income summary account. The expense and revenue accounts are closed in to Income Summary as described for a sole proprietor. However, the profit or loss will be transferred to two or more accounts rather than a single account. The Income Summary, like the drawing accounts, will be closed out for the period.

Partnership profits and losses may be divided in any manner the partners agree upon. In general, a partner may be expected to share in proportion to the amount of capital and/or services he or she contributes. In the absence of a clear agreement, the law provides that all partners share equally, regardless of the differences in time devoted or capital contributed.

Fixed or capital basis. Profits and losses are generally divided equally, in a fixed ratio, or in a ratio based on the amounts of capital contributed by each partner.

Example 11.4

Alex and Ben have capital balances of $30,000 and $20,000, respectively. The net income for the first year of operations was $15,000. If the partners have decided to share on an equal basis, the journal entry for allocation of the net income will be

Income Summary	15,000	
Alex, Capital		7,500
Ben, Capital		7,500

If, however, capital investment is to be the determining factor, the entry would be

Income Summary	15,000	
Alex, Capital		9,000
Ben, Capital		6,000

Interest Basis. Under this method, each partner is paid interest on his or her capital investment, and the remaining net income is divided in a fixed ratio or on some other basis. Thus, a partner's share depends *partially* on his or her capital investment.

Example 11.5

Instead of the equal split as in the above example, each partner is to receive 6 percent interest on his capital balance, with the remaining net income to be shared equally. The entry would be

Income Summary	15,000	
Alex, Capital		7,800*
Ben, Capital		7,200

*Alex = $30,000 × 6 percent = 1,800
Ben = $20,000 × 6 percent = 1,200

Salary Basis. The partners may agree to give recognition to contributions in the form of services, while the remaining net income may be divided equally or in a fixed ratio.

Example 11.6

Assume that the partnership of Alex and Ben agrees that a yearly salary allowance of $4,000 be given to Alex and $3,000 to Ben, the balance to be divided equally. The entry would be

Income Summary	15,000	
Alex, Capital		8,000
Ben, Capital		7,000

Salary plus interest basis. Here, services rendered to the business and capital contribution jointly determine the income division. Each partner gets a salary and, at the same time, interest on capital. If any balance remains, it is divided in an agreed-upon ratio.

Example 11.7

Alex and Ben decide to allow a credit of 6 percent interest on capital balances, respective salaries of $4,000 and $3,000, and equal division of the remainder. The entry would be:

Income Summary	15,000	
Alex, Capital		8,300
Ben, Capital		6,700

Corporations

Equity Accounting for the Corporation

Accounting for the corporation is distinguished from accounting for the sole proprietorship or the partnership by the treatment of owners' (stockholders') equity, which in the corporation is separated into *paid-in capital* and *retained earnings*. The reason for this separation is that most states prohibit corporations from paying dividends from other than retained earnings. Paid-in capital is further divided, and so we have two major capital accounts.

Capital stock. Corporate capital stock is evidenced by stock certificates. There are a specified number of shares of stock authorized by the state, generally at a specified par value. No-par stock also can be issued in most states. When stock is issued at a price above par, the amount above par is premium. If stock is issued below par, the difference is termed discount. If only one type of stock is issued, it may be termed capital stock, or, specifically, common stock. Capital stock that has been issued, fully paid, and reacquired, but not cancelled, is called treasury stock.

Retained earnings. Retained earnings represent stockholders' equity that has accumulated from profitable operations of the business. Generally they represent total net income less dividends declared. Retained earnings result only from operation of the business; no entries for transactions involving company stock are made to the account. The account is debited for dividends declared and credited for net income for the period. At the end of the year, Income Summary is debited and Retained Earnings credited for net income.

Summary

1. If there is a credit balance in the Income Summary account after closing, then a(n) _____ has been made for the period.
2. When the proprietor invests $10,000 cash in the business, the debit is to Cash and the credit is to _____.
3. A business operated for profit by two or more co-owners is called a _____.
4. The price at which the stock of a corporation is selling on the stock exchange is the _____ of the stock.
5. The two principal sections of the stockholders' equity section are _____ and _____.

Answers: 1. Profit; 2. Capital; 3. Partnership; 4. Market value; 5. Paid-in capital, retained earnings

Solved Problems

11.1 The capital accounts of Allie and Hallie have balances of $35,000 and $25,000 respectively. The articles of copartnership refer to the distribution of net income in the following manner:

1. Allie and Hallie are to receive salaries of $9,000 and $6,000, respectively.
2. Each is to receive 6 percent on her capital account.
3. The balance is to be divided equally.

If the net income is $32,000, (a) determine the division of net income and (b) present the entry to close the expense and income summary account.

SOLUTION

(a)

	Allie	Hallie	Total
Salary	$ 9,000	$ 6,000	$15,000
Interest	2,100	1,500	3,600
	$11,100	$ 7,500	$18,600
Balance	6,700	6,700	13,400
Share of net income	$17,800	$14,200	$32,000

(b)

Income Summary	32,000	
Allie, Capital		17,800
Hallie, Capital		14,200

11.2 Baggetta and Cohen have capital accounts of $20,000 and $40,000, respectively. The partners divide net income in the following manner:

1. Salaries of $10,000 to Baggetta and $12,000 to Cohen.
2. Each partner receives 5 percent on his capital investment.
3. The balance is divided in the ratio of 1:2.

Determine the division of net income if net income is (a) $34,000; (b) $22,000.

SOLUTION

(a)

	Baggetta	Cohen	Total
Salary	$10,000	$12,000	$22,000
Interest	1,000	2,000	3,000
	$11,000	$14,000	$25,000
Balance	3,000	6,000	9,000
Total share	$14,000	$20,000	$34,000

(b)

	Baggetta	Cohen	Total
Salary	$10,000	$12,000	$22,000
Interest	1,000	2,000	3,000
	$11,000	$14,000	$25,000
Balance	−1,000	−2,000	−3,000
Total share	$10,000	$12,000	$22,000

11.3 What entry is needed to record the issuance of 10,000 shares of capital stock at $40 par value? In what section of the balance sheet would this information be placed?

SOLUTION

Cash	400,000	
Capital Stock		400,000

Cash is a current asset, whereas Capital Stock would appear in the stockholders' equity section.

11.4 On December 10, 19X8, the directors of the Jordan White Corporation declared an annual dividend of $2 per share on the 6,000 shares of capital stock outstanding. What entry is needed to record the above information? How is Dividends Payable treated on the balance sheet?

SOLUTION

Dec. 10 Retained Earnings	12,000	
Dividends Payable		12,000

The dividend becomes a current liability when declared and appears as such on the balance sheet.

Chapter 12
REPETITIVE TRANSACTIONS AND PAYROLL

IN THIS CHAPTER:

✔ *Repetitive Transactions*
✔ *Use of Special (Subsidiary) Ledgers*
✔ *Use of Special Journals*
✔ *Discounts and Returns*
✔ *Payroll*
✔ *Summary*
✔ *Solved Problems*

Repetitive Transactions

In earlier chapters, the accounting principles discussed were illustrated in terms of small businesses with relatively few transactions. Each transaction was recorded by means of an entry in the general journal, then posted to the general ledger.

Such a system becomes altogether too slow and cumbersome when transactions in various categories occur by the hundreds or thousands

each month. In that case, it becomes more practical to group the repetitive transactions according to type (sales, purchases, etc.) and to provide a *special journal* for each type. Entries that are not of repetitive nature, such as corrections, adjusting entries, and closing entries, will still be entered in the general journal.

The advantages of using special journals where there are numerous repetitive transactions are:

1. **Reduces detailed recording.** In the special journal, each transaction is entered on a single line designed to provide all necessary information. Individual posting is eliminated, as only the totals from the journal's columns are posted to the general ledger at the end of the month.
2. **Permits better division of labor.** Each journal can be maintained by a different person. This not only allows specialization for the employees, but it also enables several people to be involved in the journalizing process simultaneously.
3. **Permits better internal control.** As noted in an earlier chapter, separation of duties is a key element of internal control. The use of special journals facilitates this.

Use of Special (Subsidiary) Ledgers

Further simplification of the general ledger is brought about by the use of separate subsidiary ledgers for accounts receivable and accounts payable. The advantages are:

1. **Reduces ledger detail.** The general ledger will be kept clean of detail information, which will be kept in the subsidiary ledgers.
2. **Permits better division of labor.** Here again, the subsidiary ledgers can be maintained simultaneously by different persons.
3. **Permits a different sequence of accounts.** The ledgers may be organized alphabetically by customer name (accounts receivable) or vendors (accounts payable), rather than in financial statement sequence, as is the norm for the general ledger.
4. **Permits better internal control.** Separating the responsibility for the subsidiary ledgers from that of the general ledger enhances internal control. The totals from the subsidiary

ledgers must agree with the balances in the general ledger accounts, called *control accounts*. Consequently, no unauthorized entry could be made in either the control account or the subsidiary ledger, as such an entry would create an imbalance.

Important!

The idea of control accounts is an important one. Any group of similar accounts may be removed from the general ledger and a control account substituted for it. The result is better internal control and more efficient data entry.

Use of Special Journals

The principal special journals are:

1. Sales journal
2. Purchases journal
3. Cash receipts journal
4. Cash disbursements journal

Each is described below, as is the relationship between the special journal and the general ledger, the relationship between the special journal and the subsidiary ledger, and that of the control account and the subsidiary ledger.

Sales Journal

The entry for the individual sale of merchandise on account is a debit to Accounts Receivable and a credit to Sales. Only sales on account are recorded in the sales journal. Cash sales normally do not require the recording of the customers' names and are recorded in the cash receipts journal, usually in daily totals.

Following is the procedure for the sales journal:

1. Record the sale on account in the sales journal.
2. Post from the sales journal to the individual accounts in the subsidiary ledger.
3. Record the posting of the individual accounts in the post reference (PR) column. A check indicates that the posting has been made.
4. At the end of the month, total the amount of sales made on account, as entered in the special journal. This total is posted in the general ledger Accounts Receivable control account and Sales.

The balances in the accounts receivable ledger may be summarized by listing each customer and the amount owed. The accounts receivable trial balance, known as the *schedule of accounts receivable*, should agree with the control account.

Purchases Journal

In most businesses, purchases are made regularly and are evidenced by purchase invoices issued to creditors. In previous chapters the entry to record the purchase of merchandise on account included a debit to Purchases and a credit to Accounts Payable. Where there are many such transactions, the labor-saving features of the special journal may be utilized. Although the basic principles of the purchase journal are the same as the sales journal, more columns may be necessary to accommodate the different types of items purchased.

For the sales journal, the schedule of accounts receivable total equaled the control account in the general ledger. In the purchase journal, the individual transactions with the creditors (accounts payable) are posted to the creditors' accounts in the subsidiary ledger, while the total is posted to the Accounts Payable control account.

Cash Receipts Journal

Transactions involving cash are recorded in either the cash receipts journal or the cash disbursements journal. Increases in cash may come from such sources as collections from customers, cash sales of merchandise, investments, and collection of principal and interest on notes receivable. The recording and posting procedures for cash receipts are as follows:

1. The total of the cash column is posted as a debit to the Cash account in the general ledger.
2. Each amount is posted to the individual customer's account. The total is posted as a credit to the Accounts Receivable control account.
3. The total of the cash sales column is posted as a credit to the Sales account.
4. Each item in the sundry column is posted individually to the appropriate general ledger account. The total of the sundry column is not posted.
5. The accuracy of the journal (equality of debits and credits) is verified by adding the totals for all credit columns and comparing the total to the cash debit column.

Cash Disbursements Journal

The cash disbursements journal is used to record all transactions that reduce cash, such as payments to creditors, cash purchases (of supplies, equipment, merchandise, etc.), the payment of expenses (salary, rent, insurance, etc.), or personal withdrawals. The cash disbursements journal procedures are:

1. A check is written each time a payment is made. Check numbers provide a convenient reference and are helpful in controlling cash and preparing the bank reconciliation.
2. The cash credit column is posted in total to the general ledger at the end of the month.

3. Debits to Accounts Payable represent cash paid to creditors. The individual amounts are posted to the creditors' accounts in the accounts payable ledger, and the total is posted to the general ledger control account at month's end.

4. The sundry column is used to record debits for any account that cannot be entered in the other special columns. These might include cash purchases of equipment, payment of expenses, and withdrawals. Each item is posted to the general ledger separately, as the total is not posted.

Discounts and Returns

Purchase Discounts

To induce a buyer to make prompt payments, a seller may allow the buyer a percentage discount. For instance, a 2 percent discount may be offered if the bill is paid within ten days, while the total (gross) amount is due within 30 days. Such a discount situation would be stated as 2/10, n/30. Thus, a 2 percent discount is available within ten days, and the total is due in 30.

Example 12.1

A sales invoice totaling $800 and dated January 2 has discount terms of 2/10, n/30. If the purchaser pays on or before January 12, he or she may deduct $16 ($800 × 2%) from the payment.

Accounts Payable	800	
Cash		784
Purchase Discounts		16

If, however, the bill is paid after the discount period (January 13 or later), the journal entry will be:

Accounts Payable	800	
Cash		800

In some cases, the terms may refer to a given number of days after the end of the month (EOM) in which the sale was made. For instance, 2/10, n/30 EOM would indicate that the total amount is due on the thirtieth day of the following month.

In still other cases, particularly when there is a substantial time lag between purchase of the goods and delivery, the terms may refer to receipt of goods(ROG). For instance, 2/10, n/30 ROG would indicate that the total bill is due 30 days after the goods are received.

Return of Merchandise

For many reasons a buyer might return merchandise to the seller for credit: damaged goods, incorrect size, color, or style, or a price other than that agreed upon. In such cases, the necessary journal entry would include a debit to Accounts Payable (with a corresponding entry in the subsidiary ledger) and a credit to Purchase Returns. The latter is a contra account to the Purchases account.

In such cases, the seller makes a journal entry that includes a debit to Sales Returns (a contra to the Sales account) and a credit to Accounts Receivable (both the control and the subsidiary accounts).

Payroll

Deductions from Gross Pay

Gross pay is determined by negotiations between the employer and the employee. Deductions from gross pay to arrive at net pay may include various taxes withheld, medical insurance premiums, retirement plan contributions, union dues, etc.

Federal Withholding Taxes. Under the federal income tax withholding system, federal income tax is collected from the employee as income is earned, rather than when the tax return is due. Thus, employers must withhold funds for the payment of their employees' taxes. The amount to be withheld is a function of the employee's filing status and number of exemptions, as declared on Form W-4.

Federal Insurance Contributions Act (FICA). The FICA tax (a combination of social security and Medicare) helps pay for federal programs for old age and disability benefits, Medicare, and insurance benefits to survivors. A combined rate of 7.65 percent (subject to change as enacted by Congress) is imposed on both the employee and the employer. Thus, the total is 15.30 percent.

The amounts withheld for either income tax or FICA represent a liability for the employer, as these amounts are required to be remitted to the Internal Revenue Service. The same is true for other withholdings, such as retirement contributions or union dues. The employer portion of FICA, however, represents an expense item for the employer, as would any matching contributions to retirement plans, etc.

Example 12.2

Moses Glass earned $580 for the week. Deductions from his pay were federal withholding, $85; FICA $44; insurance premiums $12; union dues $18. Net pay is calculated as follows:

Gross pay		$580
Federal withholdings	$85	
FICA	44	
Insurance	12	
Union dues	18	(159)
Net pay		$ 421

The journal entry to record the payroll would be:

Wages expense	580	
Federal income tax withheld		85
FICA withheld		44
Insurance premiums payable		12
Union dues payable		18
Cash (or wages payable)		421

There would be an additional journal entry to record the employer's portion of FICA:

Payroll tax expense	85	
FICA payable		85

The Payroll System

The payroll system generally consists of input data (for example, individual time cards), a payroll register (to compute the payroll each pay period), individual earnings cards (a separate record for each employee), and a procedure for recording the payroll and the related employer taxes with appropriate liabilities. Most payroll systems now are completely computerized.

The payroll entry is generally recorded in the general ledger, using the payroll register for the input data.

Note!

Employers must accrue payroll expenses and liabilities at the end of each pay period.

Unemployment Taxes

In addition to their share of the FICA contributions, employers are also required to pay unemployment taxes to both the federal and state governments under the Federal Unemployment Tax Acts (FUTA) and the State Unemployment Tax Acts (SUTA). Under current legislation, the tax is imposed only on the first $7000 of each employee's earnings. Although the typical state rate is 5.4 percent, rates vary depending on the state, the nature of the business, and the employer's record of unemployment experience. The federal rate is currently 6.2 percent, but employers who are current with their state tax are allowed an automatic credit of 5.2 percent, regardless of the state tax actually paid. This tax, of course, represents an expense item for the employer.

Summary

1. The journal used to record sales of merchandise on account is the _____ journal.

2. The sale of merchandise for cash would appear in the _____ journal.

3. It is common practice to divide the ledger in a large business into three separate ledgers, known as the _____, _____, and _____ ledgers.

4. The total of the sales journal is posted at the end of the period as a debit to Accounts Receivable and a credit to _____.

5. The only column in the purchases journal that will not be posted in total at the end of the period is the _____ column.

6. Sales Discounts and Purchases Discount appear in the _____ as reductions of Sales and Purchases, respectively.

7. Terms of 2/10, n/30 on a $750 purchase of January 4, paid within the discount period, would provide a discount of _____.

8. Accounts Receivable and Accounts Payable in the general ledger may be classified as _____ accounts.

9. Merchandise purchased on account would be entered in the _____ journal.

10. Merchandise sold on account would be entered in the _____ journal.

11. Merchandise sold for cash would be entered in the _____ journal.

12. Merchandise purchased for cash would be entered in the _____ journal.

13. Equipment purchased on account would be entered in the _____ journal.

14. The amount of federal income tax withheld from an employee's salary is based upon the employee's _____ and _____.

15. The two types of payroll taxes imposed on an employer are _____ and _____.

16. The payroll tax expense entry is recorded in the _____ journal.

17. The one tax usually paid by the employee and matched by the employer is _____.

Answers: 1. Sales; 2. Cash receipts; 3. General, accounts receivable, accounts payable; 4. Sales; 5. Sundry; 6. Income statement; 7. $15; 8. Control; 9. Purchase; 10. Sales; 11. Cash receipts; 12. Cash disbursements; 13. General; 14. Filing status, number of exemptions; 15. FICA, unemployment; 16. General; 17. FICA

Solved Problems

12.1 What are the net proceeds of goods sold on March 10 for $750, terms 2/10, n/30, if payment is made (a) on March 18? (b) on March 22?

SOLUTION

(a) $750 (2% = $15
        $750 ($15 = $735
(b) $750 (the discount period ended March 20)

12.2 What entries are needed for parts (a) and (b) of Problem 12.1?

SOLUTION

(a)	Cash		735	
	Sales Discount		15	
		Accounts Receivable		750
(b)	Cash		750	
		Accounts Receivable		750

12.3 An invoice for $859.78 dated August 10 offers terms of 2/10 ROG. The shipment of goods arrived on September 29, and the bill was paid on October 8. Find the amount due.

SOLUTION

We must first determine whether the bill was paid within the discount period. Since the terms are ROG (receipt of goods), we use the delivery date as the first day of the discount period. The last date for discount is October 9. Since the bill was paid within the discount period, the discount applies.

$$\text{Net cost} = \text{List price} \times \text{complement of discount}$$
$$\$859.78 \times (100\% \times 2\%) = \$859.78 \times 0.98 = \$842.58$$

12.4 Record the following transactions in the cash disbursements journal.

Mar. 1 Paid rent for the month, $320 (check 16)
7 Paid J. Becker $615 for his February invoice (check 17)
10 Bought store supplies for cash, $110 (check 18)
15 Paid salaries for the first half of the month, $685 (check 19)
23 Paid B. Cone for February invoice, $600 (check 20)
30 Paid salaries for the second half of the month, $714 (check 21)

Cash Disbursements Journal   **CD-1**

Date	Check No.	Account Dr.	P.R.	Cash Cr.	Acct. Pay. Dr.	Sundry Dr.

SOLUTION

Cash Disbursements Journal   **CD-1**

Date	Check No.	Account Dr.	P.R.	Cash Cr.	Acct. Pay. Dr.	Sundry Dr.
Mar. 1	16	Rent Expense		320		320
7	17	J. Becker		615	615	
10	18	Store Supplies		110		110
15	19	Salaries Expense		685		685
23	20	B. Cone		600	600	
30	21	Salaries Expense		714		714
				3,044	1,215	1,829

12.5 Jennifer Ford worked 44 hours during the first week in February of the current year. Her pay rate is $5.50 per hour. Withheld from her wages were FICA (7.65 %), federal income tax ($31.00), and hospitalization ($9.00). Determine the necessary payroll entry.

SOLUTION

Salary Expense	253.00*
FICA taxes	19.35
Federal Income Tax Payable	31.00
Hospitalization Payable	9.00
Cash	193.65

*40 hours × $5.50 = $220.00 (regular)
4 hours × $8.25 = $ 33.00 (overtime)
Total $253.00

Index

151